From Britain With Love

World War II Pilgrim Brides Sail to America

GW00643208

Vera A. Cracknell Long

Denecroft Publishing, New Market, Virginia

From Britain with Love
World War II Pilgrim Brides Sail to America

Denecroft Publishing
Post Box 1155, New Market, Virginia 22844

Library of Congress Catalog Card Number:
99-94615

ISBN 0-9645977-0-5 Paperback

Revised edition
Printed in the United States of America on acid free paper

To Charles who was right.
"This is for keeps."

ACKNOWLEDGMENTS

This book is a revised and expanded version of my 1988 Individualized Study project at George Mason University, Fairfax, Virginia. At that time, I benefited from the guidance of Dr. Ralph C. Baxter, Dr. Martin B. Cohen, Dr. Evelyn Littleton Pugh and Dr. Robert E. Pugh, whose help I greatly appreciated. Later, when my husband joined the SHAEF (Supreme Headquarters Allied Expeditionary Force) Veterans Association, I was delighted to meet nearly a dozen more war brides from Britain and decided to get their stories. This I did by means of questionnaires and letters.

To all those World War II GI brides and grooms who graciously consented to share their experiences and photographs with me, I extend a hearty thank you.

I owe a special debt of thanks to Dr. Ralph C. Baxter, whose guidance and help continued when he consented to make editorial comments to this new copy.

Deep appreciation goes to Ann Backway Gratz, an experienced editor who provided me with valuable assistance and support.

Many thanks to Cynthia Long Adams, Eileen Wright Karten and Sara Powell Long for their advice and expert help when needed.

I sincerely thank the following: Robert Dorang for his interest and useful analysis; William Lahman, editor of the *SHAEF Communiqué*, for printing and layout suggestions; Ronald L. Smith, archivist, The *Queen Mary*, Long Beach, California, for his research assistance; and John Gratz, who skillfully executed the book cover design.

Cheers to my wonderful husband, Charles, for his word-processing expertise and patience--except when expressing a few colorful expletives--but mostly appreciation and thankfulness for his loving support and encouragement.

CONTENTS

****

FOREWORD

I had only recently arrived at *20/20* in 1986 when I was assigned what sounded like an intriguing story: a reunion of GI war brides in England that autumn. Like most Americans who had grown up with deep appreciation for—but little firsthand knowledge of—the sacrifices made in World War II, I was eager to report on this very special piece of our history. But I had no idea how the story would capture my heart. It was an extraordinary event, with uncommon heroes, whose tales will resonate for generations to come. And I still cry every time I re-screen the tape and hear Dame Vera Lynn start to sing. The other Vera who made it all work is Vera Long, who, with her husband, Charles, provided elegance and humor to this fascinating slice of our past. How lucky for everyone that she has written it all down! At a time when scholars are finally acknowledging that history is more than battles fought and kings crowned, this account of the war brides is a valuable addition to our heritage.

Lynn Sherr, 1996
ABC News 20/20
New York, NY

PROLOGUE

England, 3 September 1939

"I'd like to wring Hitler's neck!" said my mother unexpectedly and very much out of character for her. That was the memorable day Britain and France signaled Hitler that he had gone too far when he invaded Poland--his latest "territorial claim"--and World War II began. Vicious war clouds had long been gathering over our heads, but I, as a carefree youngster blithely engrossed in my own small world at the time, would not realize the full significance of the day until later.

September's weather that Sunday morning was particularly mild and sunny, but inside our house the atmosphere bore a serious electric air that I found puzzling when I came to the breakfast table. My widowed mother was preoccupied, seemingly glued to the wireless, and my usually teasing sisters were quiet. I was pleased and soon buried my nose in the Sunday comics, forgetting about Sunday School.

Our old marble clock on the mantelpiece chimed eleven. "Prime Minister Chamberlain is to speak," said Mum. Her sweet and kindly face was tense as she listened intently to the broadcast from Downing Street. The shocking news soon came. We were at war with Germany!

"Oh! The poor young lads who will have to go off to fight. That villainous Hitler has a lot to answer for," she muttered with tears in her eyes.

Suddenly a whining undulating siren pierced the air and captured our attention. AIR RAID WARNING! Was the unthinkable about to happen?

We all jumped up and dashed outside to investigate. Our red-bricked terraced house was on a small quiet cul-de-sac on the outskirts of London. The window panes of most of the houses already sported strange looking strips of brown paper pasted in a crisscross fashion to protect them against the blast of bombs--"if the worst came to the worst," and some blackout curtains had been hung. All our neighbors seemed to have had the same urge to gather outside, sharing the same shock and uncertainty of what would happen next.

"I can't see anything. Can you?"

"Shouldn't we put our gas-masks on?" yelled Terry Moore, the curly-hair boy who lived next-door-but-one and was a horrid bully sometimes.

He was referring to the nasty, rubber-smelling monstrosities that the government had recently issued to us.

The morning's blue and friendly sky still looked innocent. Huge roses growing in tidy front gardens, in upturned bloom, peered at us over iron chain-links (soon to become wartime scrap metal) that hung decoratively between brick-posts. Their peaceful and familiar appearance was reassuring. Suddenly, a loud voice exploded above the still-wailing alarm.

"Get back inside!" It was the usually taciturn man from across the street, Mr. Windmill, who limped from an old World War I wound and usually scowled at us if we played too close to his manicured garden. I was amazed to see his waving arms, his ruddy mustached face and balding head so vitally animated.

"You **know** it's dangerous to stay on the street. Take cover at once!" he barked in an unexpectedly military fashion.

That was enough for me. I had been sufficiently frightened by the unknown demon Hitler and his doings. Running madly back inside the house, I flung myself into the small cupboard-under-the-stairs and hid. I usually disliked this dark and spooky little oblong place, with Mum's mops and brooms propped up on the walls, but now it seemed to be a safe haven. I dared not stir for fear that some unknown devastation would engulf me.

There I stayed until returning footsteps sounded in the hallway. The tempo and scale of family chatter indicated that things had somehow returned to normal. My mother's worried voice drifted by.

"Where on earth can that girl be?"

I was now feeling rather ashamed, but before I could move the cupboard door was flung open by one of my excited sisters who peered inside and triumphantly yelled, "Here she is. What a cowardy-custard."

"I'm NOT!" I answered, as I rather sheepishly rejoined the family.

"The all-clear sounded. It was a false alarm," they tauntingly chorused.

That evening, when helping to close our blackout curtains, I climbed up on a chair to better reach the top. Getting down in the darkened room I stepped the wrong way, caught my foot in the arm of the wooden chair, and toppled down to the floor with a bang, bringing the chair with me. Hitler got me that day after all. It looked as though I'd broken my ankle.

The next day an ambulance came to take me to Wembley Hospital to have my foot X-rayed. "You don't need a stretcher," Mum told one of the ambulance men coming to the door. "She doesn't weigh seven stone yet. Just pick her up and carry her." I was suddenly SO embarrassed (and mad at my Mum) as one of the young men swept me up and carried me out. Luckily, my "war injury" turned out to be a badly sprained ankle, but that was painful enough.

A year later, during the heavy air-raids, my sister Joan and I were almost evacuated to our Aunt Pat in California under a government-sponsored scheme for sending youngsters to Canada and America. Tragically, on 17 September 1940, a German U-boat attacked a convoy in the Atlantic and sank the *City of Benares,* drowning nearly ninety of the children aboard. The transatlantic evacuation plan was soon abandoned by the British government.

"We'll stick together," said Mum, who hadn't really been too keen on sending us so far away from home in the first place.

The war continued and our London neighborhood received its share of Luftwaffe blockbusters, delayed-action bombs, incendiaries, V-I robot bombs ("doodle-bugs" to Londoners) and V-II rocket-propelled bombs-- Hitler's "Vengeance Weapons," the last of which zoomed down in March 1945. Our house sported rows of strafing bullets, lodged above bedroom windows, from swooping aircraft flying overhead. Incendiary bombs had fallen on our roof. Neighbors helped one another amid feelings of a shared camaraderie. As time wore on, everyone seemed to become more fatalistic and desensitized to any danger. "If your name is on the bomb, there's nothing you can do about it!" What would be, would be.

September 1945. World peace at last.

After six years of war, my initial fright in 1939 was barely remembered. We had grown up fast during those embattled and tumultuous war years. Youth had no chance to be bored and impatient for some kind of action or thrill when each day brought one crisis after another. Happily, the urge for young people to fall in love thrives in any circumstance, and in the midst of those uncertain days it happened to me and a tall good-looking American soldier. Later, when peace swept in a new era, it became possible for him to return briefly to England on leave. And wedding bells!

America beckoned me again, and this time I really would sail there.

Vera A.C. Long

During the Second World War GI (GI JOE) became the popular name for an American soldier.

**Sgt. Long, U.S. Army
France, 1944**

GI: (Government Issue or General Issue). Widely used by the U.S. Armed Forces to designate clothing, supplies, such as: GI boots, GI soap, GI haircut.

The *GI Bill* (Public Law 346, 22 June 1944) provided benefits that helped veterans adjust to civilian life; with unemployment payments, housing loans, college education, insurance and the "Fifty-Two Twenty Club." Twenty dollars a week for up to fifty-two weeks, if unemployed.

The term "GI BRIDE" was first expressed in England.

INTRODUCTION

From Britain With Love
World War II Pilgrim Brides Sail To America

A light upon the shining sea—
The Bridegroom with his Bride!

Alfred, Lord Tennyson, *St. Agnes' Eve*

Only once, in 1945, has the United States Congress passed special legislation to expedite the admittance to America of thousands of immigrant girls. In early 1946 the first in a fleet of modified troopships sailed from Southampton, England, carrying war brides and babies to New York: a flotilla "wondrous strange."

Before the 20th century dawned, international marriages were confined to the wealthy and those arranged for political, dynastic or economic reasons. During the 1900s, however, two devastating World Wars, in spite of their shocking horrors, facilitated love and marriage between thousands of servicemen and the girls they met while serving overseas.

American **Doughboys** in World War I had married and brought home 8,000 European brides. The **Yanks,** directly after World War II, brought home over 100,000 war brides, nearly two-thirds of whom came from the British Isles. Even a few "male war brides" were included, showing the new independence of servicewomen. In the following postwar Occupation and Cold War years, American troops stationed in countries throughout the world continued to bring home many more foreign brides with them.

Although the World War II migration to America of GI brides began covertly while the war was still being fought (a few thousand young women paid their own fares and sailed "space available" in convoys), the majority of the brides had to wait for official government action. This came about on 28 December 1945 when the 79th United States Congress passed the *War Brides Act* (Public Law 271). This act allowed, within a three-year period, alien spouses and children of U.S. service personnel and honorably discharged members of the armed forces to be admitted to the country as nonquota immigrants for permanent residence.

Most of these GI dependents were in Europe, and the War Department gave them priority by converting a fleet of over thirty troop and hospital ships into passenger vessels with nurseries. In January 1946 the first of these specially prepared GI bride ships was readied, and a contingent of British dependents set forth on a voyage from Southampton to New York. Southampton was the U.S. Army's major European port of embarkation for the war brides until eventually Le Havre and Bremerhaven became ports for transporting Continental European dependents to America. Early in 1946, over in the Pacific, plans were made to ship over 8,000 Australian, New Zealand and Philippine dependents to San Francisco.

Altogether about 70,000 British GI brides sailed across the Atlantic to America while another 40,000 of their sisters went to Canada as brides of Canadian servicemen. "The Petticoat Pilgrims" was the way a London newspaper man described the sailing of the war brides from Southampton. He wrote that it was "the strangest of all pilgrimages" because it consisted of women. They were following in the footsteps of their early 17th-century Pilgrim ancestors.

English brides had set a precedent nearly four-hundred years earlier, when the first contingent had sailed to the New World. Those were the "maydens" for Jamestown, Virginia. In 1619 women were scarce in the struggling English colony, and more families were needed to help the budding settlement stabilize and grow. Families were the keystone to social order and stability, and only the wealthier planters could afford to bring wives with them. Perhaps the first Anglo-American marriage took place when John Rolfe married Princess Pocahontas after she learned English, embraced Christianity and took the name Rebecca. But that marriage was an exception. Shrewdly, therefore, mercantile officials of the Virginia Company in London organized and sponsored the sailing of one-hundred forty "warranted chaste and honest" maidens to settle on Virginia's soil. In 1620 they arrived in Jamestown amid much rejoicing, welcomed by lusty bachelor-farmers.

Centuries later, in 1946 at the close of World War II, a different, more personal love story was unfolding, but similar expressions of joy re-echoed against the backdrop of New York City's skyscrapers--and San Francisco's Golden Gate Bridge--as each GI bride ship edged slowly into port.

As it turned out this large-scale migration across the high seas brought the last significant group of settlers to arrive in America while the restless and mighty oceans still represented a frontier-like barrier between the Old and New Worlds. The sense of finality shared by those young girls--when it took their ships many days or even weeks to navigate the vast and tempestuous ocean--is difficult to imagine now in today's jet and space age. Going to America in the 1940s seemed like going to a new planet, and the brides, some as young as sixteen, wondered if they would ever see their families again.

These World War II pilgrim brides were unique also because, contrary to the common ethnic settlement pattern of immigrants who stuck close together in certain communities, they immediately spread out across the country to countless cities and hamlets. They went to wherever their husbands lived and added their own cultural heritage to the local blend of Americana. They had to come to terms with their new environment and economic situation, which pleased some and greatly shocked others, while picking up the threads of married life with their GI grooms--who looked somewhat different wearing civilian suits or overalls!

Some girls discovered that their new in-laws spoke little English or none at all. The reality of meeting this hurdle was even more surprising to them because their husbands had always sounded and acted so typically American. Department of Justice records for 1941 showed that some five million people living in the States at that time did not speak English or know basic facts about U.S. history and government. Americanization classes for adults had been introduced a few decades earlier when the need for such sessions was first perceived, and millions of immigrants had benefited from the program. Their children were able to attend local schools and soon blended into society, but it was much harder for the older generations to change. The Second World War saw their sons march off to serve, and, when they returned, some of them brought home another "foreigner." These families would have preferred that their sons marry local girls with the same ethnic background as theirs.

Occasionally, religious differences proved to be a problem. At a dance early in 1944, held at the Hans Crescent service club in London where Kathleen "Kick" Kennedy (daughter of former ambassador, Joseph P. Kennedy) served as an American Red Cross girl, I was puzzled when a GI friend suddenly asked me what I thought about Kick's upcoming marriage to the Duke of Devonshire's son. "They're in love. Why not?" I naively asked. Because "she's Catholic and he's Protestant," he replied. Coming from a small, mainly Protestant country, some British girls who married Jews or Catholics were distressed at the rough time they had in being accepted by their American in-laws. Some never were. Sometimes having children helped. The Puritans had sought religious freedom for themselves in America, so had others. But in the twentieth century, religious problems were something the girls had not foreseen.

Recently, it was observed that the GI war brides "are a part of the war we don't read about in American history books." For example, in one military history book which is devoted to the collective experience of the American GIs in World War II, only buried within parentheses is the bare fact that over 100,000 of them got married overseas. Why was that considered so unimportant when men had fought for democracy and freedom of **choice**? Out of the evils of war had come love. Those overseas marriages had a higher success rate than comparable wartime U.S. marriages. They helped nurture stable families, ethnic understanding and boosted social as well as cultural exchanges.

Of the original war brides, those who met their husbands abroad during the war, the majority came from Great Britain, and it is mainly their story that is explored in the following pages, narrated by women with firsthand experiences. Canadian war brides, British war grooms, a French girl who worked for the U.S. Army and a war baby also contributed their experiences. The British spouses, who were sometimes told they spoke "good English for a foreigner," generally were not perceived to be newcomers when compared to non-English speaking emigrants. They shared social, literary and political roots with America which made their transition that much easier. Despite this, when it comes to being completely assimilated into American culture, almost all new immigrants instinctively cling to a few of their Old Country ties and loyalties for life.

Once described by some disapproving elders as "those naughty girls who go out with the Yanks," most of them today are grandmothers and even great grandmothers. All are "Old Age Pensioners" or "Wrinklies," as senior citizens are commonly called back in Britain. How many GI brides were there? For many reasons, the number differs even in official sources.

Time has marched on, and this collection of oral histories gives a glimpse of bittersweet international romances from World War II: courtship, marriage, journey to America, first vivid impressions and how they fared in the new land. What has endured from these relationships? More than memories. For most GI marriages, like the old "spreading chestnut trees" where we grew up (and played conkers with the horse chestnuts), it is our heritage and offspring that will continue to grow and spread out across this vital land.

Data have been gleaned from the stark records of Congress, the United States Center of Military History, the Immigration and Naturalization Service, the National Archives, the American Red Cross, the Imperial War Museum in London, books, magazines and the news media, but chiefly from war brides' oral histories gathered over several years. Old photographs engagingly highlight most narratives.

Sadly, a few of the participants have died since sharing their stories, but their memories remain.

"Here is my journey's end," William Shakespeare.

1

1939-1945: THE WAR YEARS

Background in Great Britain

We weren't ready for war, you know, but Hitler was. By 1940 the Germans had reached the English Channel. Churchill announced that there would be no church bells rung until the end of the war, or, if we heard them tolling a knell, we'd know that Germany had invaded England.

Margaret Hill, Oral history tape, 1983.

So reminisced an English mother while visiting the home of her daughter, Margaret Skibiak, in America. None could have guessed how lives would be changed by the war or where destiny would eventually send them. Anyone who lived in the British Isles through those perilous years after Britain and France declared war on Germany, 3 September 1939, would never forget the stress and danger from the threatening Nazi war machine as it systematically began to devour anything that stood in its way. This is what they remembered.

Adolf Hitler, Führer and Chancellor of the German Third Reich, had previously marched into Austria and Czechoslovakia, making his usual ethnic "territorial demands" and on 1 September 1939 he invaded Poland. Britain and France had pledged aid to Poland, so they immediately entered the war, but with Hitler's lightning land-and-air-blitzkrieg and with the unexpected appearance of the Russian Red Army to the east, Poland was overwhelmed and fell.

The world had been astonished only a month earlier, August 1939, when Hitler and Joseph Stalin had signed a non-aggression pact, but now the true significance of this agreement became evident when Stalin gobbled up his half of Poland for Russia.

Hitler now paused. In the early months of 1940 some American newspapers were calling this a "Phony War!" Not for long though because the

German blitzkrieg started on its destructive warpath again when Hitler pounced on neutral Denmark and Norway to get harbors for German ships and U-boats. Then on to Holland, Belgium and Luxembourg, so as to engineer a round-about-way into France, thus avoiding the "impregnable" Maginot Line. Paris fell. Stalin, who had already over-run Finland, chose this time to invade other Baltic neighbors. On 10 June 1940, Italian Fascist leader, Benito Mussolini, also jumped at his opportunity to wage war against Britain and France, lashing out at allied forces in North Africa.

In the British Isles, an invasion by Germany threatened the country after the fall of France and the desperate sea rescue of nearly 350,000 of the British Expeditionary Force and other allied troops from Dunkirk. On 4 June 1940 the new Prime Minister, Winston Leonard Spenser Churchill, told Parliament that the epic evacuation across the English Channel carried out by the Royal Navy and thousands of brave civilian boat-owners, was a miracle of deliverance. But "wars are not won by evacuations," he warned. In Germany a boastful Hitler on 19 July 1940 predicted that England would now sue for peace after accepting his military triumphs, and that Churchill would "flee to Canada." Not likely! Churchill's leadership at this time was invaluable in stirring Britain to fight on with nothing more than "blood, toil, tears and sweat." He was called a war-monger by some and the Germans hated his bull-dog resolve, but, as John F. Kennedy later put it, Churchill mobilized the English language and sent it into battle! Indeed, the **Battle of Britain** was nigh.

In the summer of 1940 Britain prepared herself for the expected German onslaught. A secret defense plan, code named *Cromwell*, would be implemented by the Royal Navy, Air Force and Army when the invasion of Britain appeared imminent. More civilian help and resources were tapped. To augment the defense of the island, nearly two million older men (up to age 65), volunteered for the Home Guard units located near their own cities, towns and villages. They trained and armed themselves with sporting guns and rifles or commandeered whatever weapons were available, including machine guns and rifles from the First World War. Young women "joined up" and went into one of the three armed forces, toiled on farms, or worked in war factories. Other civilians volunteered as air-raid wardens, firemen, Women's Voluntary Service, Red Cross, or helped in a myriad of other ways. Everyone on the Fortress Island would be in the front-line of battle, and they all "did their bit," as the popular phrase went.

Air-raid and gas mask drills were carried out in schools and other public buildings. On 26 June 1940, Churchill warned Duff Cooper, his Minister of Information, that

> the Press should handle air-raids in a cool way without undue prominence or headlines. The people should be accustomed and treat air-raids as a matter of ordinary routine . . . as if they were no more than thunderstorms.

Hitler plotted to invade and occupy Britain by September 1940. He called his proposed invasion *Sealion,* and its success would depend upon establishing German mastery of the sky over the English Channel. Hermann Goering, Commander-in-Chief of the superbly trained Luftwaffe, fresh from victories over Poland and France, was arrogantly confident of a swift victory over Britain. But first, Flight Command of the Royal Air Force (RAF) had to be smashed. Goliath was ready to strike down David. This, however, the valiant RAF Spitfire and Hurricane fighter pilots never allowed. Their morale was high under the leadership of Air Chief Marshal Sir Hugh Dowding, who had implemented new lines of communications that vastly helped the pilots by linking radar and Royal Observer Corps stations with Ground Control. Orders thus went directly from RAF Headquarters at Bentley Priory to the various airfields. In the shortest possible time, small groups of fighters would "SCRAMBLE," already knowing where to find the "bandits." They were fighting over home ground and had learned to use effective aerial tactics. Dowding made important and correct strategic battle decisions, so that the young fighter pilots ultimately gave Britain a crucial victory. Churchill told the British people:

> Never in the field of human conflict was so much owed by so many to so few.

This was the first aerial battle effectively using a high-tech radar control system, and winning the Battle of Britain was to prove a major pivotal victory for the Allies.

Aggressively, meanwhile, the mighty Luftwaffe's Heinkel and Junker bombers, escorted by Messerschmidts, carried out indiscriminate terror bombings on London, hoping to break the spirit of the British people. Waves of German planes darkened the skies above and left bright, blazing

1940: Barrage Balloon and Anderson Shelter in the foreground.

1944: Piccadilly Circus, London. The statue of Eros was removed and the pedestal boarded up for the duration of the war.

infernos below. The people suffered, but they prided themselves in carrying on. Signs saying "Business as usual," appeared in front of badly damaged shops and buildings. Hitler had not reckoned on their Churchillian tenacity.

Edward R. Murrow's nightly transatlantic radio news broadcasts from the British capital, "This is London," with his vivid descriptions of the Blitz and its fiery devastation, struck a sympathetic cord with his attentive audience back home in the U.S.A. as they gathered around and listened to the family radio. As Archibald MacLeish poetically said when telling Murrow what power his verbal images had:

> You burned the city of London in our houses and we felt the flames that burned it.

Many daring young American men went to Canada and volunteered to help Britain, some by serving in the American Eagle Squadron of the Royal Air Force. Gallant pilots and crews from the Dominions and Colonies already served, seeing action in British skies along with expatriate French, Polish, Belgian, Dutch, Czech and other nationals who had escaped from Nazi conquered lands to wage war from British bases.

Winter approached, and with it came fog and worsening weather. Hitler's 16 July 1940 order to prepare for Germany's invasion across the English Channel was postponed until the following year. By the end of 1940 Hitler conceded that his air assault could not crush the Royal Air Force. But attacks from the air causing extensive civilian casualties and destruction from increasingly sophisticated bombs, would continue until the end of the war in 1945 when the last scary bolt-out-of-the-sky, V-II rocket-propelled bomb, exploded in London. No time for an air raid warning to sound with those missiles on the way! It was only four minutes from take-off to impact. One survivor described hearing a loud "ripping sound, then a **wooshing** rush of air--like a giant drawing in a deep breath," followed by a strong concussion and smoking ruins. Hitler's secret weapons warfare on Southeastern England lasted nearly a year, from June 1944 (after D-Day when the first V-I pilotless Flying Bombs were launched from the Pas de Calais), to early April 1945, when the last of the V-II rockets were fired from Holland.

Five years earlier, in 1940, the London Blitz was about to begin. Britain desperately needed more "tools" to fight with, and Churchill appealed to America, still officially neutral. Franklin Delano Roosevelt listened and came to the rescue by proposing Lend-Lease legislation during a late 1940 Christmas holiday "Fireside Chat." The President shrewdly used a neighbor helping neighbor analogy to that of America aiding Britain--"you lend your hose to your neighbor if his house is burning but you don't first ask him to pay for it." Roosevelt continued by declaring: "We must be the great arsenal of Democracy."

Ultimately, helping Britain was deemed vital to the defense of America, and a determined Congress, fighting the country's isolationist element, passed the Lend-Lease Act that went into effect 11 March 1941. At about the same time, over in Britain, the coming of Spring meant intensified bombing raids, rapidly growing in scope. Harbors, port cities and non-military areas were targeted. The ancient cathedral city of Coventry was flagrantly incinerated and destroyed. In a twelve-month period, from June 1940 to June 1941, nearly 100,000 civilians were killed or seriously injured.

On a much broader front, the Battle of the Atlantic accelerated as Germany tried to starve Britain into submission with a strangle-hold sea blockade and prevent her from receiving much needed supplies of food, raw materials and other vital goods from overseas. Churchill said gravely:

> At home we must face the war against the U-boat torpedoes, Focke-Wulf Condor bombers, the continuing Blitz and the invasion threat.

The Atlantic Ocean battle of attrition was the longest continuous deadly struggle of World War II. Providentially, by 1940 British cryptanalysts succeeded in cracking the German *Enigma* ciphers and codes. *Ultra*, their code name for the top secret intelligence derived from this marvelous breakthrough, was one of the Allies' greatest successes of the war. The ability to read German *Enigma* messages proved especially invaluable in their winning back control of the Atlantic Ocean. *Ultra* intelligence enabled the Allies to divert convoys away from German U-boats while directing escort naval hunter-groups toward the hidden prey to destroy the enemy. But still, in 1940 and the early years of the war, the scale of the horrendous Battle of the Atlantic was tipped in favor of the elusive submarine U-boats. A dreadful toll was paid in sunken British and Allied ships and many thousands of seamen's lives.

By mid-1941 it became evident that Hitler's top priority to send his invasion forces across the English Channel had drastically changed when he abruptly turned and concentrated his power on an invasion of Russia (Operation *Barbarossa*), thereby breaking his "friendship" pact with Stalin. Hitler had decided that the invasion of Britain could wait another year, until the spring of 1942, by which time he imagined that "the Russian campaign will be completed." Hitler was too optimistic. His Operation *Sealion* never did take place after furiously fighting Russians pushed back the German invasion, and Russia became Great Britain's powerful ally. Overlapping these momentous events in Europe, on the other side of the world in the Pacific, Japan's imperialistic war schemes were racing to a shocking end-of-year climax.

Without warning, on 7 December 1941, a Japanese naval and air task force savagely attacked the United States naval base at Pearl Harbor on Oahu Island, Hawaii. The surprise raid, which took place even as Japanese diplomats conferred with officials in Washington, D.C. about resolving differences between the two countries, was costly in American lives and crippling to the U.S. fleet. "A treacherous and unprovoked attack," said President Roosevelt, "a day of infamy," and America immediately declared war on Japan. Following Pearl Harbor, Germany and Italy declared war on the United States. Japan had earlier (27 September 1940), signed a Tripartite Pact with the Axis powers, Germany and Italy. So the stage was set for Americans to bear arms in World War II. For Britain, this now meant they would receive more than U.S. Lend-Lease aid, valued as it was. Additional fighting men were sorely needed before the Nazi and Fascist powers in Europe could be quashed and Japan's imperialistic ambitions could be vanquished.

Operation *Magnet* was the code name for sending the first American troops to the United Kingdom. They landed in Belfast, Ulster, Northern Ireland. Ulster shared with the rest of the United Kingdom in being targeted by German planes, and in 1941 Belfast suffered very heavy bombing.

On 26 January 1942 the first group of 500 soldiers from the 34th U.S. Infantry Division arrived in Ulster, soon to be followed by many thousands more. Little known was the fact that about 1,000 American civilian technicians had gradually and quietly preceded the soldiers' arrival by many months in order to build U.S. naval and air bases. Belfast's harbor, geographically the most westerly area of the U.K. provided valuable means of protection, fuel and supplies to transatlantic ships and convoys that faced the perils of the Atlantic Ocean. The U.S. Navy operated from its Londonderry base in Ulster for most of the war. Ports in Eire, the Republic of Ireland to the south, were denied to the Allies because of its neutrality throughout the war. Furthermore, the Axis powers were free to keep their Legations and nationals in Eire, and this posed a serious security threat to Ulster and to Britain across the Channel. President Roosevelt considered it a "danger to the lives of American soldiers and to the success of Allied military operations." In 1942, *A Pocket Guide to Northern Ireland* issued in Washington, D.C. warned GIs:

> Axis agents send out weather reports, and find out by espionage what is going on in Ulster. The Ulster border is 600 miles long and hard to patrol. Axis spies sift back and forth across the border constantly.

Eire's Prime Minister, Eamon de Valera, continued to be insensitive to the Allied cause when, even as the horrors of the concentration camps: Buchenwald, Auschwitz and others were becoming known, he visited the German ambassador to offer sympathy on hearing of Hitler's death. During the war, nevertheless, many Irishmen from the South crossed over to Britain and joined their cousins to fight the Nazis.

Lend-Lease in reverse was put into play when Churchill offered the swift giant liners *Queen Mary* and *Queen Elizabeth* for transporting American GIs to Britain. The "famous GI Shuttle" from New York to Gourock, Scotland began in the spring of 1942. It was the first time a ship had sailed with 10,000 people aboard. Then on 2 August the total was upped to 15,125 troops and 863 crew (nearly an entire army division) on the *Queen Mary*, known as the "Grey Ghost" in her wartime make-up, as she speedily zigzagged safely across the Atlantic. Thereafter, huge contingents that peaked at 16,683 men and supplies continued to arrive on the *Queens*. Others were packed into a variety of smaller vessels including the numerous American Liberty Ships, hastily built for that very purpose.

Over the next few years the constant flow of troops and equipment from the United States continued. The Army Air Forces, Infantry, Armored and Airborne Combat Divisions, special units and the U.S. Navy arrived. Britain, as the last free bastion against Nazi fascism and located near the Continent, was already crammed with thousands of fighting men and refugees from many of the conquered nations. Sometimes whole families from nearby Low Countries, like Belgium, managed to escape to England across the Channel before it was too late. More than a million

GIs passed through Britain, staying only a few months or weeks, while en route to other theaters of operation, including North Africa and Italy. But another one-and-a-half million GIs came and were stationed, on the average for two years, in the British Isles. Many of these Americans were soon actively participating in the war, along with the RAF, on bombing-raids over the Continent. The U.S. Army 8th Air Force had arrived in May 1942, and three months later the first huge B-17 Flying Fortresses took off from their British bases for enemy territory. Eventually, it took 127 airfields to meet the needs of the "Mighty Eighth" by transferring some facilities from the Royal Air Force and by plowing up precious farming acreage and building new airfields, mostly in the flat, picturesque Constable countryside of East Anglia, an area about the size of Delaware. Later, the 9th U.S. Army Air Force was formed and arrived overseas well in advance of the D-Day invasion that it was designed to support.

During World War II, probably for the first time in history, two sovereign nations, Great Britain and the United States, agreed to share their top secret cryptanalytic know-how in their global conflict against the Rome-Berlin-Tokyo Axis aggressors. The Strong-Hastings BRUSA agreement in 1943 officially provided for this "Special Relation."

Since 1940, at Bletchley Park outside of London, an ingenious electro mechanical "Bombe" (*Turing Machine)* created by mathematical wizzard Alan Turing and named after the earlier Polish "Bomba" device had made it possible to find the keys to *Enigma* ciphers by testing the cryptanalysts' hypotheses (cribs). Keys varied with radio nets and were changed daily or even more frequently. When a key was solved, decoding of a message could begin. By 1943 the production of *Ultra* intelligence at Bletchley involved thousands of people. Data recorded on five-level (teletype) paper tape was transported thirty feet on spools through an electro-mechanical "computer," named *Colossus,* for decoding.

What was known to very few was that, while Bletchley Park's cryptanalysts worked around the clock producing *Most Secret Ultra* intelligence, American soldiers were doing likewise at 59 Weymouth Street in London, a few blocks from Grosvenor Square and HQ/ETOUSA (Headquarters, European Theater of Operations, U.S. Army). *Most Secret* became *Top Secret* after the Americans entered the war.

One of those GIs recalls "machine processing" the surreptitiously acquired *Enigma* enciphered military codes:

SGT. CHARLES LONG:

In August 1943 our IBM unit arrived in London, joining the Signal Intelligence Division (SID) operations on Weymouth Street under Colonel George Bicher.

Early on, in Washington, the U.S. military had concluded that it must increase the volume and speed of its communications intelligence production. The possibility of using IBM data processors to ferret out cryptanalytic keys and manipulate data for decoding was investigated.

Long before every thing with bits (binary digits) in bytes (eight bits to a byte) was called a *computer,* IBM was the world leader in the field of Automatic Data Processing (ADP). When World War II began, IBM ceased marketing its systems abroad, and by 1942 its production of new ADP equipment was available for **lease*** only to the U.S. Government and for only the highest priority military use. The Signal Intelligence Service, located at Arlington Hall, not far from the Pentagon, had the necessary priority, and in 1943 some of the newest type IBM machines and twenty-four data processing technicians were sent to London.

We joined HQ/ETOUSA's Signal Intelligence Division there and installed our state-of-the-art IBM machines in the basement at 59 Weymouth Street. It proved to be a significant advantage having an IBM Section to help expedite the processing and decryption of voluminous *Enigma* signals. Starting in September 1943, we made exhaustive tabulations, frequency distributions and permutations of intercepted *Enigma* enciphered five-letter word groups around the clock. Our daily priority was to process the *F-Traffic.* We compiled data as requested by our cryptanalysts upstairs and regularly updated and printed lists of Call Signs being used by the Luftwaffe pilots (Birdbook) and the Wehrmacht (Elephant Book). All of our output was labeled <u>Top Secret *Ultra.*</u>

The production of *Ultra* intelligence was increased in 1944 when U.S. Army Signal Intelligence Detachments began using smaller improved "Bombes" made by NCR (National Cash Register) in the United States to assist the cryptanalysts at GCHQ (Government Communication Headquarters) in Bletchley Park and at HQ/ETOUSA.

After D-Day our operation moved to Paris and then on to Germany, concentrating on Russian communications.

---

*IBM did not **sell,** only **leased,** its machines which sorted, selected data, etc., and performed mathematical functions.

The year 1944 was crucial for Britain and her Allies in the fight to free Europe from Nazi Germany's grip. Early that year the tempo of Allied military combat maneuvers accelerated, particularly in newly designated "off-limits" rural areas. Along the coast, naval, aerial and special forces training intensified. Britain now teemed with an inflated population and the deadly machines of war.

The wags joked that the overcrowded island was in danger of sinking except that it was being held up by the countless cable-tethered **barrage balloons** that dotted the sky and horizon! The cables, attached to the huge gas-filled balloons, served as a defense against dive-bombers and machine-gun strafing by low-flying enemy planes. People took comfort in seeing the fat barrage balloons aloft, as well as hearing the ear-splitting ack-ack (anti-aircraft) guns during air-raids, while at night bright searchlights swept the skies.

By Spring 1944 all of southern England became a vast staging area for *Overlord*, the long awaited D-Day assault that would begin on the beaches of Normandy. Civilians living in English coastal villages and hamlets were quietly evacuated while the incoming combined Allied sea, land and air forces mobilized for the liberation of France and the defeat of Germany. It was to be the biggest invasion force the world had ever known: 7,000 ships, 11,000 aircraft and 3,000,000 men from Allied nations mustered to breach Hitler's "Atlantic Wall" of artillery and fortifications that stretched from Norway to Spain. Early in June, a fierce north-westerly gale and torrential rain threatened a successful launching of the invasion, and Supreme Allied Commander, General Dwight David Eisenhower, delayed the landings for twenty-four hours. Then, with a lull in the weather predicted by staff meteorologists and a brief conference with his chief Allied commanders at Southwick House near Portsmouth on the South Coast, Ike gave the vital D-Day order when he said "OK. Let's go." Four years in its planning, the long awaited invasion was ON! General Eisenhower told the troops:

The eyes of the world are upon you. The hopes and prayers of liberty-loving people everywhere march with you.

With the epic invasion of Europe underway, the huge armada of ships and aircraft with men and matériel aboard embarked from English shores. Airborne paratroopers and gliders were among the first to land in

Normandy while, submerged in the waves close to the beaches, Royal Navy four-man midget submarines waited to act as beacons for the incoming landing-craft. Field-Marshal Sir Bernard Montgomery, Ground Force Commander, who believed that "meticulous preparation, balance and the morale of troops was everything" when going into battle, showed his own confidence in the operation by bringing with him a Rolls Royce, sans camouflage! Monty, a popular hero with the people, trusted by his troops after leading them to victory at El Alamein and the defeat of German forces in North Africa was, according to Churchill: "In defeat unbeatable, in victory unbearable."

It would take the Allies eleven months of resolute fighting, much bravery, personal sacrifice and heartbreak, however, before gaining Victory in Europe. May 8th 1945. Then those Allied forces prepared to go to the Pacific and join in the fight against powerful, fanatic Japanese forces. Fortunately, in August 1945, the dropping of the atom bomb brought Japan's surrender. After nearly six years of war, **world peace**, at last.

Back in Britain before D-Day, 1944, when the American "occupation" of those islands was in full swing, not unexpectedly, many a local British lass and American GI had fallen in love and married. In fact, one of the first weddings was performed in April 1942 when Herbert Cooke wed Thelma Smith in Belfast, Northern Ireland. Many other couples became engaged "for the duration," hoping to be safely reunited after the war. And eventually tens of thousands of determined couples overcame the military regulations aimed at discouraging overseas wartime marriages. Then, the happy pair still faced many real and emotional hurdles before they would be able to "set up housekeeping" together (American colloquial saying of that time).

In retrospect, it is hard to imagine that an American serviceman when being shipped overseas on his way to unknown wartime dangers in "this man's army," would have had any thoughts of finding serious romance, let alone actually getting married abroad. But such were the fortunes of war. Moreover, such were the moral and social values of the 1940s that it was expected of any honorable soldier to marry the girl that he courted and loved.

At the same time, U.S. Army officials did their best to protect GIs from getting serious with "guileful" girls.

"GEE HONEY, YOUR HAIR SMELLS SO SWEET"

So said a Yank while dancing slowly with an English girl at the popular Hammersmith Palais de Danse in London. What a way to get a pretty girl's attention and interest. Most Englishmen would never think of saying such a thing. Yet the newcomers from over-the-seas with a different "line" were in a class by themselves in more ways than one.

Probably no other expeditionary force in history had been given more generous and protective care by its government than the United States military in World War II. These American servicemen were better paid, fed and clothed than any others, and, reflecting their New World brashness, had more than their rightful share of self-esteem and confidence. What a jolting contrast these fresh young-bloods made to the harried natives in Britain (and later on the Continent) who had grown used to the darkness of war, bombs, disasters and extreme shortages.

Early in the war Britain had become the first country to conscript women for a variety of vital war services. The young male population had long since been called to the colors, and the British Tommies (and their British Dominion and Commonwealth comrades) had rallied around the flag of freedom against Nazi tyranny. By 22 May 1941, all eighteen-year old British girls had to register for conscription. They were usually called up for service before their twenty-first birthday, but many girls did not wait for this to happen and volunteered for the service of their choice. This freed more British men for fighting overseas with the armed forces. In 1942, as the Yanks began to arrive from the U.S.A. and as more men in the British forces were being sent abroad to North Africa, to the Middle East and Far East, the time was ripe for giving young GIs and British girls, born thousands of miles apart, a unique and unexpected opportunity to meet one another.

Enter the friendly gum-chewing Yanks dressed in their smart two-piece uniforms, which made the ranks and officers look almost alike, except that the army officers wore giddy pinkish trousers. Gwen Bradley Scruggs lived in Basingstoke, Hampshire as a young girl, and she remembers the newcomers. "They were handsome and dashing in their uniforms, chewing gum--they were just exciting." In towns and villages GIs had a field day dispersing gum, chocolate bars and sweets (all severely rationed in

Britain) to curious children who soon learned to yell, "Got any gum, chum?" to which the knowing GI's replied, "Got any sisters, mister?" One way or another they met the local girls. Instant rapport.

Perhaps General Dwight D. Eisenhower, when he arrived in London early in May 1942, set the pattern of mutual harmony between American men and British women after meeting Kay Summersby, the driver who had been loaned to him. In the course of time, Summersby was assigned to the General, became a WAC officer, and served as Eisenhower's close and invaluable secretary and personal assistant for the rest of the war.

There has been much speculation about the personal relationship between the General and Summersby. Historian and Eisenhower's biographer, Stephen E. Ambrose, believed that, " . . . loving Mamie did not necessarily preclude loving Kay" during those crisis-packed, oft'times lonely, wartime years. General Omar N. Bradley wrote in his 1983 auto-biography, *A General's Life*, that "Ike had become excessively pro-British in his attitudes and thinking." Bradley and others believed that "his close association with Kay and her family" contributed to Ike's attitudes and that Kay's "influence over him was greater than is generally realized." One officer remembers that everyone knew that Kay was Ike's "P.A!" While in Paris, Ike gave Kay a letter, dated 22 August 1945, asking the American Ambassador in London for help in securing an American visa for Kay, who was to be in the city for only one day. Whatever "emotional involvement" there was between them, however, it was doomed to end in the realities of peace, the strict moral and social climate of the 1940s, Ike's post-war ambitions and his love of Mamie and family.

When the Americans were first arriving in wartime Britain, Eisenhower realized that "our friendly invasion" was bound to produce friction with the civilian population in its quest for training grounds, airfields, naval ports and accommodations for nearly two million men, plus storage and handling facilities for mountains of supplies. After all, Ike pointed out, the whole of the British Isles is only slightly larger than Colorado. The General also felt that psychologically the Americans believed they were freedom's savior come to help Britain get out of a hole; while the British public looked upon itself as the real savior of democracy. For over a year, they were the "only unbreakable opponent of Nazism," standing alone on their sceptered isle against all odds until help arrived. Both feelings were well-founded.

Another potential problem was the behavior of the GIs in Britain. Their introductory knowledge of the country was provided by films, talks and a 38-page handbook, *A Short Guide to Great Britain* by Eric Knight, produced jointly by the War and Navy departments in Washington, D.C. Knight noted the common history shared by the two English-speaking countries--and then listed some "do's and don'ts" in order to avoid mutual misunderstandings.

Margaret Mead, the anthropologist, believed that GIs in Britain should be warned that the American concept of a "date" was not the same thing over there as it was back home. She had been sent to England to study the cultural and courtship habits of the natives and reported to the Office of War Information that she feared GI morale would suffer because of the differences. Mead believed that British boys dated only girls they were serious about, or if they had some "ulterior motive, good or bad." Otherwise, they went out with "the boys" to enjoy a pleasant evening. She thought that when American boys went out on a date, it was for "something pure and beautiful," and to have an evening of fun with the girls.

Additionally, Mead reported, the absence of flirting and back-chat among British teenagers was astonishing to Americans, and that wisecracking Yanks "with a line" were very confusing to the girls. Some were insulted by the speed and assurance of a GI's approach while others took his words for serious wooing and expected a wedding band to follow his ardent declaration.

Yet another big problem, according to Mead, was the lack of comfy front porches on the homes where the couple could sit and laugh together on an American type date that "exists for itself." Nor were there drugstore soda fountains to go to for soft drinks and jukebox music. Instead, the British loved to walk and relax in parks, and many members of the opposite sex would go to pubs to drink beer and the like. That was "quite unsuitable" for young GIs. It was organizations such as the American Red Cross that provided the suitable places Mead wanted for GIs where they could socialize and dance with the kind of nice girls "mothers wouldn't worry about." And have coffee with American-style donuts, too.

In another vein, a U.S. Army officer on the scene believed that British women were not used to the deference shown to them by American men. He said this was a tradition that was ingrained in the souls of American men since the pioneering days when women in the "Wild West" and backwoods were scarce. After all, women had not only shared the everyday hardships and dangers of homesteading, but the hazards of repeated childbirth drastically reduced their life expectancy. And in the 1940s, for various other reasons, America's population still numbered more men than women.

Certainly the girls were impressed by the good manners of many GIs. Alma, a young girl living in the countryside of Norfolk, was one who admired them, explaining that they were so courteous and polite. "They held your coat, they pulled your chair out for you when you sat down. We'd never seen any of this before." One of the gallants, George Lackey, impressed Alma so much that she fell in love and married him.

A more down-to-earth broadside for the GIs was called *How to Stay Out of Trouble*, issued April 1943 by the Provost Marshal, it dealt with the dangers of exposure to wanton "Piccadilly Commandos" and the like. Prostitutes were just what many servicemen were hunting for, but brothels were illegal in Britain, and the rape laws were very strict. By 1943, there was a growing problem with the spread of venereal disease (VD) as nearly 2,000 cases of gonorrhea and a couple hundred cases of syphilis and other infections were reported among American servicemen. One Londoner remembered her embarrassment when, with her boyfriend, they both tried to avoid looking at the glaring black, red and white VD warning posters displayed in the Underground "tube" stations.

An age-old scourge, the VD problem would grow in 1944 and become even worse after the troops reached the Continent. The U.S. Army attacked the problem by dispersing information and taking remedial measures. Films were shown to GIs, cartoon-type VD warnings appeared in the *Stars and Stripes*, and pamphlets, such as "Army Talks: VD" were printed. Condoms ("strippers" or "rubbers") were freely available to the men as well as instructions in sex hygiene. Prophylactic treatment, as well as physical "short arm" inspections, were common. By 1944, the GI Pro-Kit, a cream medication consisting of sulfathiazole and calomel, was an effective VD treatment if used soon after contact with a streetwalker.

The new miracle drug of the times, Sir Alexander Fleming's antibiotic penicillin, was a precious commodity but in very short supply because of stringent production conditions and the growing demand for its use. Top priority went to battle casualties, but it became available to VD patients whenever possible.

Prostitutes on the prowl were one thing, but the changes and upheavals of war had produced an increase in the number of so-called "good time girls." More girls were leaving their home town to work elsewhere on the war effort. In doing so, they enjoyed a lot more independence and less parental control. Simply put, they toiled hard each day in a variety of jobs, and afterward some of the girls wanted to go out and have a gay (meaning *lively* in that era) time. Some were married women with husbands serving overseas for many years. Whatever, they found their matching number amongst the thousands of GIs, with money to burn and sometimes dangling impossible-to-get nylon stockings, who were out hunting for girls just like them.

Not surprisingly, the illegitimacy rate in Britain during the war reached its highest point since the years after the First World War. Abortions were illegal at the time and furtive back-street arrangements to have one were both expensive and dangerous. Pregnant girls found that collecting any future paternity allowance from an "unwilling" GI was virtually impossible. He was well-shielded by the U.S. Army.

One American, Sergeant Thomson, found himself in the news after fathering quadruplets by a British woman, Nora Carpenter. When his wife back in the States refused to divorce him, the army stepped in and quietly reassigned him to another area. Little Nigel, Ben, Colin and Peter joined the approximately 20,000 illegitimate GI babies that were born in Britain during the war. In one town north of London where GIs had been stationed for a long time, a road sign warned them to, "Please drive carefully, that child may be yours." Many of these children would be raised in British orphanages because the mother could not cope alone or for other reasons. American help and generosity apparently dried up once unwanted babies appeared. Even a soldier's contribution (allotment) to support his wife and family was a completely voluntary matter.

Black soldiers were a novelty in 1942 Britain, and they experienced a new freedom among the people there, many of whom had never seen a black person before. Children found the black GIs just as generous as the white soldiers, perhaps even more so, when giving away treats like candy and gum. Girls who loved to dance, to jitterbug and jive were willing partners for the black soldiers on the dance-floor. Others found them very polite and rather fascinating. They were different.

The American Army at that time was a "Jim Crow" army and strictly segregated. This posed something of a problem to the British government because there was no way that civil or military authorities could assist in carrying out U.S. segregation policy. No law-abiding person could be prevented from entering a public place and certainly not because of his color. To cut down on potential trouble, the U.S. services rotated leaves and passes to something like a "Blacks Tuesday, Whites Wednesday" policy for nearby dances and other social recreation. The ever popular pubs (public houses or inns) and even fish and chip shops in some towns and villages were sometimes delegated "black" or "white" by the military.

Some white GIs were outraged at the sight of a black soldier consorting with a white girl, and violent incidents were known to have flared up in different parts of the country. Black GIs were stabbed, shot, even castrated as rumor would have it. The worst incident was in 1944 near a pub in Newbury, Berkshire when a roaring gun fight between white and black GIs resulted in the deaths of a local woman and two black GIs.

The army discouraged blacks from dating the local white women and getting serious. It usually denied them permission to marry. This was probably wise if the GI was from one of the nineteen states, mostly in the still segregated South, that prohibited mixed black and white marriages. Hundreds of mixed-race babies were born to couples who often had gained parental blessing to marry but not the permission of the military. Only after the war was this kind of discrimination addressed, but not halted.

It was not until 26 July 1948 that President Harry S. Truman in Washington, D.C. signed Executive Order 9981 expressly giving "equality of treatment and opportunity for all persons in the armed services without regard to race, color, religion or national origin."

For thousands of young couples things were taking a potentially serious path. Many a GI was taken home "for Sunday afternoon tea" to meet the girl's family. Sometimes the romance was shortened by the demands of war or just fizzled out; however, when love bloomed and steadily deepened in those days, marriage was **the** next step. That was very serious business, ordained by church and expected by society to protect young women. Having a baby out of wedlock was considered shameful to the "fallen" girl and her family. Certainly a heartless stigma for the child.

American troops had been cautioned not to get serious with the local girls. It was thought that some women would use their wiles just to get a one-way ticket to Hollywood-land. Prudently, therefore, the U.S. Army's policy toward the overly ardent soldier was designed to discourage him from thoughts of marriage. Many GIs were very young, they had never been so far away from home before, and the uncertainties of the times made it easy for romance to thrive.

The parents of young girls were worried too. Fathers were especially strict and stopped more than one romance. An Essex girl remembers a GI boy friend who promised to write after he left, but she never heard from him again. Years later, after her father died, she found old letters from the soldier that her father had hidden from her.

MARRIAGE BY THE NUMBERS

Wartime letters always seemed to arrive in bunches, and one day in August 1945, when the postman delivered several from my Yank stationed in Germany, one envelope stood out larger and thicker than the others.

Greeneyes . . . now I must get you to fill out your part on the enclosed U.S. Army forms. Also, I've written a letter to Lottie asking her to please "put it in writing" that she gives her permission for you to marry me (Ah!). The Army needs **four** original forms. Love ya Button-nose, Your Red Wolf.

We had met in London and parted a year earlier. Before he left for France, we had exchanged love tokens. He had given me his gold high school ring engraved with the letter K (Kingston, Pennsylvania). It was cut at the back and squeezed together to fit my finger. I had given him an old silver ring embossed with a tiny deep-blue butterfly wing, that fitted his little finger. Now we were thankful that World War II had ended victoriously for us, for the Allies. After writing to each other every day and with the war finally over, we were anxious to get married. We also knew that it would be easier for me to join him in the U.S.A. if I was his wife, not just his intended bride.

Still, my mother was rather shocked when the Army's papers and his officious sounding request for my hand in marriage arrived. How my resolute Yank would manage to get from Germany to England and then back to join his military unit before its imminent return to the States was another story. But it all happened as we had dreamed it would.

Roadblocks set up overseas during the war to protect any GI who showed intentions to marry included interviews with a commanding officer, talks with a chaplain, much official paperwork, investigations, and generally a two-month waiting period. Some chaplains believed there should be even more red tape before allowing overseas marriages to take place. One GI was moved to ask officialdom, after going through the process, "Did it ever occur to you, sirs, that we are in love with our intended wives, just as much as we would be if they were Americans?" Despite the Army's admonishment then, a couple still intent on matrimony had to proceed by the numbers:

Under the provisions of Cir 41, HQ European Theater of Operations U.S. Army, dated 17 April 1944, as amended by Sec. IV, Cir 89, HQ ETOUSA, dated 14 August 1944 and Letter WD, file: AG 291.1 (11 Sept 43) OB-S-SPGAL-M, subject **Overseas Marriage Of Military Personnel**, dated 24 November 1943, which I have read and thoroughly understand, the following is submitted:

1. Soldier's Declaration of Intention to Marry.
2. Fiancée's Letter of Acquiescence.
3. Parent's written approval (for persons under 21 years old).
4. Chaplain's consultation with the soldier.
5. Fiancée's personal interview by the soldier's Commanding Officer or chaplain (where feasible).
6. 1st Ind(orsement) of approval: Investigation of both parties show no impediments to the marriage.
7. 2nd Ind. of approval: Joint income of parties sufficient.

Letters and forms had to be filled out in triplicate, unless otherwise stated. No carbon or mimeographed copies accepted, thank you. For most, the earnest-minded couples, it was worth it, and eventually their marriages were approved:

8. Permission to marry after a further 60-day waiting period.
9. Investigation reveals that both parties are eligible to marry, and that such marriage will **Not Bring Discredit to the Military Service**.

How abashed the sparkle-eyed bride and her soberminded parents would have been if they had been privy to such official United States army jargon. The aspiring bride was informed, nevertheless, that her marriage to an American soldier would

NOT confer United States citizenship upon an alien . . . although it does facilitate the alien's later entry into the United States and naturalization after taking up residence there.

NOT confer special privileges including Commissary, Post Exchange, government quarters, medical or dental services.

Her marriage would entitle her to U.S. Army allowances, insurance and other benefits as authorized by law. Once the soldier-groom could obtain a three day pass or a longer furlough, the couple were free to wed.

10. Final approval for arrangements to be made for a future civil or church wedding. Comply with church or civil authorization to marry.

The Church of England required that those wanting to be married in their local Parish Church must have the banns called by the Curate for three consecutive Sundays. So it was that **our** names had been called for the third time. I thought it sounded funny listening to our banns and hearing myself being called a "spinster" of the Parish. And I had silly visions of poor *Jane Eyre*: the bit in the story where after the final banns had been read and the marriage ceremony was about to take place, a figure from across the seas suddenly appeared with "just cause" to stop the wedding. Vivid imagination aside, all was in readiness **if** my GI groom could "make it to the church" any time before he had to sail home to America.

It was now late October 1945, and the weather had turned nasty, cold and rainy. We heard reports on the wireless of gales blowing over the English Channel. No one could possibly cross from the Continent in that weather. It was tea-time and we had just sat down at the table when the front doorbell rang. Amazingly he was there waiting on the step--and ready to catch me up in his arms. Two hectic and exciting days later we were married on a blessedly Indian summer day. No time to round up all my war-scattered family which caused one of them to grumble, "You could have knocked me down with a feather when I heard that she had wed!"

There are always exceptions-to-the-rule, and a few GIs with ulterior motives bypassed the "blessing" of the U.S. Army and simply married gullible young girls in civil marriage ceremonies--sometimes because the man already had a wife in America. One air-gunner from Michigan (later killed on a mission) was found to have had a wife back home, one in London and a third in King's Lynn. It was discovered that he had a child by both "wives" in England. Hopefully, the American grandparents were told about their son's offspring overseas after he was killed.

A legitimate child of an American citizen GI with full legal rights could easily gain U.S. citizenship when the baby's birth certificate and other relevant papers were registered with the American Embassy or at an American Consulate's office. A tolerant Congress lowered the minimum legal age requirement from twenty-one to eighteen, so that children of younger soldiers would have their citizenship safeguarded. The baby was then eligible for an American passport. Not so the baby's mother.

The GI brides themselves would have to reside in the States for two years before being able to apply for American citizenship although this residency requirement was dispensed with under a provision of the law for foreign spouses of military personnel still serving overseas. The British war brides had retained their British citizenship though married to an American (or another foreigner) but would lose it automatically when becoming a citizen of another country. That is, however, until **Dual Nationality** became possible on 1 January 1949 (when the *British Nationality Act of 1948* went into effect). Since that date, British born persons who became naturalized citizens of another country no longer lose their British nationality. To give up their British nationality they have to make "a formal declaration of renunciation in front of a British Consul or other British official" authorized to accept such declarations. For sentimental reasons, not very likely.

Girls who married during the war and then were anxious to get to America faced difficult problems in getting permission to cross the Atlantic. Strict visa requirements and other official controls then in effect made the process extremely slow. Visas were valid for only four months at a time. But the biggest hurdle of all was gaining a berth on a ship. Sometimes the brides went on a standby basis on hospital or prisoners-of-war ships and sailed when spaces were available. A letter of 26 May 1944 from the Adjutant General's office in England spelled out the existing law and wartime policy of the United States government concerning this matter:

> The wife will not be transported at Government expense for the period of the war and six months thereafter. However, the English wife, if not likely to become a public charge, may enter the United States as a **nonquota** immigrant at any time after marriage if transportation facilities are available and the parties have private means for payment thereof.

An "Affidavit of Support" filed by the husband or his family in America was required. The effects of The Great Depression, which were still prevalent in the States at the start of World War II, meant that many GIs still supported older parents back home and had allowances for them deducted from their pay. It was seldom easy to fulfill the American

Government's list of requirements. Having a foreign-born wife was something of a luxury.

Amazingly, with the Battle of the Atlantic still underway, several thousand women and children succeeded in crossing the torpedo-menaced ocean on Allied ships whenever space was available. A few never reached America because their ships were attacked and sunk. The actual number of brides (aliens) and children (recognized as U.S. citizens) who arrived before the end of 1945 is hard to gauge. According to the 26 November 1944 *New York Times*, over 400 brides had arrived from Britain and other parts, and they were joined that day by 80 new brides from Australia and New Zealand. American Red Cross records show that by the end of 1945 (before the official U.S.Army's scheme for transporting GI brides and children to America went into effect) over 5,000 brides had reached the United States. Historian Norman Longmate puts the figure at 30,000 but his figure includes those who were "in the pipeline" and actually sailed later. Even harder to gauge is the total number of war brides.

According to the U.S. Department of Justice, Immigration and Naturalization Service, there were about 38,000 British war brides who entered the country under the December 28, 1945 *War Brides Act*. Obviously, not all of the war brides were counted at that time because the Department of the Army Military History, detailing the "shipment" of the GI brides in 1946, said that "as of 26 April 1946, a total of 45,814" United Kingdom applications had been received, with another "4,600 expected before the end of June." Numerous human factors stood in the way of an orderly "shipment." Pregnant women had to wait until six months after the birth of their babies before applying and sailing. Sometimes their GI husbands returned to live with them in the U.K. for several years. War widows and those being divorced had to make their own travel arrangements--not an easy task in those chaotic postwar years, so they usually ended up staying at home. Also, a lot of GI husbands had reenlisted, and according to U.S. Army transportation records they had "advised their wives to delay departure until they knew whether or not they would be assigned to the European Theater." In July 1946, their records show that 9,356 U.K. dependents were still awaiting transportation to America.

Among those not counted in the mainstream war bride and groom statistics were a number of British service personnel and civilians who married Americans in the United States during the war. Such were the destinies of Annie MacRae, Royal Navy; Gilbert Braithwaite, Royal Air Force, and Patricia Grimshaw who arrived to marry the GI she had previously met in London. The setting for their love stories adds a different perspective to those wartime Anglo-American marriages which took place on the other side of the ocean.

A British WREN Goes to New York

During the Second World War Annie MacRae from Elgin, Morayshire, Scotland served four years in the Women's Royal Naval Service (WRNS or "Wrens"). In 1943 she was sent to America to help modify Lend-Lease planes for the Fleet Air Arm of the Royal Navy. It wasn't long before a sailor in the U.S. Navy, Lawrence Stapp, wanted to change the course of Annie's future life.

Years later, Annie still retains her quiet, lilting Scottish accent and ready smile.

1943: Annie MacRae in the Royal Navy.

ANNIE:

I came over to America in March 1943 on a Canadian ship, *Empress of Scotland.* There were fourteen of us Wrens, originally thirteen, so they hurriedly grabbed another girl to make it fourteen. Then we were supposed to sail on Friday the 13th, but we couldn't do that, so we sailed very early the next morning. The U-boats were a dangerous threat, so we had to dodge around quite a bit. We reached New York in ten days.

We were stationed at Roosevelt Field on Long Island, where Charles Lindberg had taken off in 1927 on his historic solo flight to Paris. They had the barracks there and the aeroplane hangars. Our orders were connected with Lend-Lease warplanes for the Royal Navy. We changed equipment on the "new" *Curtis Seagull* planes and called them *Seamews.* We took some American equipment off and put on the British equipment we had brought with us.

An article in *The Boston Daily Globe* dated 2 August 1943 said that while the legislation permitting WAVES to go overseas waits for Congressional action, "British Wrens in N.Y. work on planes." The article by Molli Oliver went on to describe that we Wrens were performing meticulous work around the planes "while wearing navy bell-bottomed trousers (measuring 27 inches around), white cotton shirts, web belts and beetle-crushing boots . . . all of them capably releasing a stout British seaman for active duty." Our dress uniform consisted of navy skirts, pea jackets, "berets" with the gold letters H.M.S. and those thick, black cotton regulation stockings that we had to wear.

We girls ate in the Mess Hall, and, when we walked there, the sailors stood outside and watched us. Lawrence Stapp was a photographer in the U.S. Navy, and he got a British sailor to introduce us. Three weeks later, Larry proposed, but I said it was too early. I didn't know if I wanted to stay or not. My parents in Scotland thought they were too far away to say much about it. I was of age, anyway. Larry took me to meet his family in Urbana, Illinois, and they welcomed me. I was in uniform and his three-year old nephew said to me, "Why are your legs black?" His father told him that I rode there in a coal-car.

We were asked to march in the Fourth of July parade in New York City. It was 1943, and I can't remember how many British sailors and Wrens there were. Some people booed from the side-

**1943: Three WRENS with an American sailor in tow,
Roosevelt Field, Long Island.**

**Annie, second from the left, received a "BOTTLE" (reprimand)
for having her uniform jacket unfastened.**

line, and I remember how amazed we were. We shrugged it off. I thought Britain is such a little country to be responsible for so much. Another time in a New York theatre the news showed the Land Army Girls working in Britain, and a man behind us clapped his hands like mad and said, "Why don't people appreciate what they're doing over there?"

Remember the song, "One dozen roses and put my heart in beside them?" Well, Larry sent me a dozen red roses with a card that quoted words from the song. He's never been so romantic since! We were married on Long Island in November 1943. Larry

> ## When I left home in March 1943, I didn't expect to stay this long . . .

was sent to Annapolis so I requested a transfer to Washington, D.C. I couldn't understand the accent of the people from the South--or the children. I remember hearing the police sirens, but I still looked up at the sky expecting an air raid. Later, Larry was sent to Florida for officer's training. Twice he expected to go overseas, but, luckily for us the war ended when Japan surrendered.

After the war, my mother came over for a visit as soon as she could get transatlantic passage. We had two daughters. I didn't go back to Scotland until 1965 (after twenty-two years) when my youngest daughter, Barbara, was five years old.

I'd forgotten, but my daughters recently reminded me that I used to call them "you little heathens!" if they were naughty. Once a neighbor told me I was always saying "Hey! Hey!" to discipline the children. She also thought it was funny because I would sit outside, very early in the spring, all bundled up, reading a book and eating my lunch in the fresh air.

My children called me "Mummy" when they were young. Marianne would say, "Look at this, Mummy" and people would turn around and stare. But they stopped along the way, and I didn't say anything. I used to think that to become Americanized you've become homogenized.

I still bake Scottish shortbread and make mince and tatties (ground-meat and potatoes). We now have a bonny granddaughter. Larry retired from his photography business, and we enjoy garden work, club activities and travel. We celebrated our Golden Wedding Anniversary in 1993. When I left home in March 1943, I didn't expect to stay this long in America, but it has been a good life, and I have no regrets.

THE ROYAL AIR FORCE "OVER HERE"

Former Naval Person* to President Roosevelt
19 May 1941.

I expect you are now acquainted with the splendid offer which General Arnold made to us of one-third of the rapidly expanding capacity for pilot training in the U.S. to be filled with pupils from here . . . the first 550 of our young men are now ready to leave . . . a second batch of 550 to follow on their heels. It will greatly accelerate our effort in the air.

*Winston Churchill's humorous cover when writing to the President.

During World War II, Royal Air Force Cadets trained as pilots in Canada and the United States. Other RAF servicemen were stationed with official delegations implementing and coordinating the program. In 1941 the U.S.A. was still "neutral," but in March, Congress approved Lend-Lease aid to its friends who were fighting Nazi Germany. Then in April, a U.S. Navy destroyer "shot in anger" at a German U-boat they believed was attacking them. America's Eastern seaboard was being haunted by hoards of ever-encroaching U-boats and warships. They lay in wait to attack laden convoys departing for Britain--easy targets silhouetted against bright lights dotted on the shore.

With the war getting close to home, on 27 May 1941, President Roosevelt declared an "unlimited national emergency in the U.S.A." Two days later, the United States agreed to establish flying schools to train Royal Air Force cadets as pilots. The U.S. government would receive $10,000 from Great Britain for each student trained.

Eventually, seven British Flight Training Schools were established in California, Arizona, Oklahoma, Florida and Texas. The first group of cadets arrived in June 1941. To keep a low public profile, and to avoid any local opposition in those early days, the British men wore civilian clothes. But that policy soon changed after Pearl Harbor, and America went to war. From 1942-1945 several thousand new RAF cadets arrived in North America for flight training.

Sadly, a few of those cadets were killed while being trained. Memorials honor their memory; their graves are in a "foreign field that is for ever England" (Rupert Brooke's war sonnet, *The Soldier*). Burial sites may be found in distant places like The British Plot in Oak Ridge Cemetery, Arcadia, Florida; or in cemeteries in Mesa, Arizona; Miami, Oklahoma; Terrell, Texas and others. In 1994 a 50th Anniversary ceremony was held at Falcon Field (named after the British bird of prey) in Mesa for the 2,000 RAF cadet pilots who had trained in Arizona. Some of the surviving pilots and instructors--all members of the Falcon Field Association in Britain--came back to Mesa for the commemorative reunion. Actor Jimmy Stewart, a former pilot in the U.S. Army Air Force, spoke at the poignant memorial ceremony. A lone British Spitfire flew overhead.

On a happier note, and not unexpectedly considering the number of Yanks during the Second World War who took brides while overseas, some of the RAF lads stationed in the U.S.A. fell in love with the girls they met there. Consequently, the Royal Air Force Register of Marriages in Washington, D.C. shows that one hundred RAF servicemen married American sweethearts during the war. One such couple was Gilbert and Luceille.

GILBERT:

I was working as an Audit Clerk in Gloucester and living with my family when the war started. I remember the air raid sirens sounding not long after the actual declaration of war was announced on 3 September 1939--fortunately a false alarm. Gloucester was spared any heavy raids, although many pots of tea were brewed until the "ALL CLEAR" was sounded! In July 1941 I was called up for service and went into the RAF. A couple of years later I sailed on the *Aquitania*, then in service as a troopship, from Gourock, Scotland and didn't have the slightest idea where I was heading.

There were about one hundred British servicemen on board from various branches of the armed forces, and we soon found out that we were going to the U.S. to be stationed around the country with different delegations. At that time, ships going on westward voyages traveled almost empty, but they were jammed packed with U.S. forces on the return trip. One of my main memories on board ship was the welcome sight of **white bread!** Wartime bread in England was basic and greyish. The trip was without incident although we had plenty of armament aboard with Royal Navy gun crews. The *Aquitania* traveled alone and relied on speed to dodge the U-boats. We arrived in New York City on 30 December 1943.

On arrival, we were regally taken care of by the Salvation Army and spent one night at their Red Shield Club. The charge was fifty cents. I remember very well that the weather was freezing cold, and our greatcoats felt good. However, on arrival in Washington, D.C. one of those typical D.C. changes in weather happened. The temperature was in the seventies, which was like a heat wave to us. Walking down Connecticut Avenue with full uniform and kitbags--you can imagine how hot it became. I was attached to the Headquarters RAF delegation in Washington, D.C. We were paid $5 a day for board and lodging, plus fifty cents a day extra for overseas allowance. We found our own place to live in one of the various rooming houses.

The American people really opened their homes to our chaps in uniform under an organization called The Home Hospitality Scheme. We had many happy occasions visiting with families, and we felt sure this was their way of showing appreciation for the way their men were being taken care of "over there." A sad occasion was when we attended the funeral service for Field Marshal Sir John Dill at the Washington Cathedral. To most of us this was probably the first large military funeral we had attended. It was very impressive and, again, showed how much the American people joined with the Mother Country to get the war over and done with.

One day in October 1944 I went on a blind date. My RAF sergeant (who had become a war groom) and his wife needed an escort for a friend to attend a sorority ball, Chi Sigma. Both of the ladies were members of this sorority and that's how I met Luceille, who became my wife. She was a G-Girl from Oklahoma-- one of the many girls who came to work for the U.S. Government during the war. I think both of us were very shy at that time, but it did blossom out to be a full romance, and we became engaged in late December 1944.

I asked my C.O. for permission to be married. It was approved, and details of the marriage were later entered in the RAF register of marriages here in Washington, D.C. My mother back in England was very disturbed at first hearing of our plans. She eventually

**1945: Luceille and Gilbert Braithwaite
enjoy springtime blossoms in Washington, D.C.**

**Luceille Sturdivant came to Washington, D.C. from Ada,
Oklahoma to work for the U. S. Government during the war.**

got over this problem when my wife finally met the family in July 1957, and then everything was lovely.

We were married 17 February 1945, at the Augustana Lutheran Church, Washington, D.C. It had snowed, and I fell down as I left my rooming house to walk to the church for my wedding. Perhaps it was a good omen! I only had three days leave, so our "honeymoon" was spent at home.

I had no trouble adjusting to the American way of life. Speaking the same language, for one thing, made the change in life style so much easier. Also the District of Columbia is very cosmopolitan with many different nationalities there. I stayed on RAF duty in Washington, D.C. until 1948 when I returned to England on the *Queen Elizabeth* for my discharge, after serving for seven years.

Under U.S. Immigration rules at that time I had to obtain a visa and a green card from the American Embassy in London before I could return to Luceille in America. She had been entitled to passage to the U.K. as my wife, at British Government expense, but instead she stayed at home, and so I was able to make a free round trip to England and back to the States. This was legal and a good thing because I wasn't eligible for U.S. Government transportation (under Public Law 271), my bride not being a servicewoman. I had to join the regular quota "queue" for would-be immigrants, and it took me six months to get my visa from the American Embassy.

After my return I started to work, in September 1948, for the *Washington Star* newspaper. Luceille was then employed at the Department of State. Except for trips to England to see my family, and going back and forth to Oklahoma (where we still maintain my wife's family home), all our married life has been spent in the Washington area. We still keep in touch with several wartime friends and often recall the war years with them and others who served in the U.K. and Europe. Through the years, my wife has become a confirmed tea drinker! We seem to stay busy since we retired doing volunteer work and, until our local branch closed down, we were very active with the RAF Association.

Summing it all up, it has been a great and lovely experience, and neither of us regrets the decision we made some fifty years ago. We both wonder how our lives would have turned out had it not been for the war. Many war brides must wonder the same thing.

English GI Fiancée Wed in Wartime U.S.A.

London 1943: Patricia Grimshaw

Pat, one of the first GI fiancées to leave England, sailed to America in March 1944 while Allied preparations for D-Day were under way. She and her sister Norma ran a family shop and two stalls on Inverness Street in Camden Town, London. During air raids she helped Fire Watch and worked at a NAAFI (Navy, Army & Air Force Institutes) Canteen in Whitehall--where she once bumped into Churchill, and then exchanged a few pleasantries! Pat met William Moran in London while he was still a civilian. Her story reflects her Cockney accent and sense of humor that, years later, have not changed.

PATRICIA:

In 1941, before America got into the war, Bill Moran was a civilian working on codes at the American Embassy in London. In those days London was right in the thick of things, front line really, with air raids and blackouts. Our house was bombed. Didn't have a proper roof for the rest of the war. Still, we had some fun. I used to go skating at an ice rink at Lancaster Gate. That's where I met Bill. I was skating around and noticed this chap in bright colors--like a bloody flamingo. Suddenly, someone in a bright red sweater comes sailing past me flat on his backside.

"That's not the way we skate over here" I told him. He gets up, sopping wet, and asks me if I would like a cup of coffee. "Don't drink coffee" I told him, "only tea." In the end we went across the street to Lyons Tea Shop and had a cup of tea.

Soon after Pearl Harbor I saw this chap coming toward me one day, smiling broadly, and I thought what a bloody cheek he has. Then I realized it was Bill in uniform, looking like a man from Mars. And with his stripes on upside down, too!

We were coming from ice skating and walking near Marble Arch, and suddenly Bill turned to me and said, "You know what? I love you and think we ought to get married." But we didn't. Bill was taken ill and they flew him back to the States. He wanted me to follow as soon as possible, but I said, "You never know, you might meet someone back there, or this might be one of those fizzling things, and I'm not going to get married and have a mess-up." We were writing for two years.

Bill wrote to Norma (our parents were dead) and asked, "Why won't Pat come over?" He told Norma that when the war ended she could come out to live with us. One day I decided to go. Bill got a priority certificate and paid my fare but I had to wait for travel orders. Finally, in March 1944 I left London for Liverpool. That was my mother's home, and I wish I'd had time to nose around, but I didn't. My mother had been a ship's stewardess when she was young, and she went to Canada and everywhere.

I sailed from Liverpool on the *Brittanica*, in a convoy. The civilian passengers aboard the ship included German-Jew refugees, scientists, and five English and American women. We called ourselves the "English-speaking union." People asked me later on if I was afraid of the U-boat torpedoes No! Instead of looking up in the sky for bombers you just looked down. It took us three weeks

> —didn't know the money, didn't know a damn thing.
> It's an eerie feeling.

to cross over. We were chased all over the place, and the convoy got broken up. We went to Boston instead of New York as we were supposed to. I asked the Captain why we'd gone to Boston and he said "Well, do you know New York any better than you know Boston?" So I had to go down to New York—didn't know the money, didn't know a damn thing. It's an eerie feeling. Bill was working in Virginia and had no idea exactly when I'd arrive. He expected me to be in New York City, so I went there by train.

First thing when I arrived I went to the Ladies Room, to the "LOO," but I couldn't open the door. "How do you get in?" I asked a big blowzy woman. "Put a dime in the slot," she answered. "What's that?" "Ten cents. You're new around here." Then she put some money in the toilet-door slot and said, "Have this one on me!" I'm sorry I didn't have time to thank her properly, but I shot inside the door and saw the toilet seat up against the wall with a glow around it. I thought, "Oh, Gawd! Don't tell me they illuminate their arses when they go to the toilet." I found out later it was a sanitized fluorescent seat.

The Travelers' Aid Society helped me find a place to stay for the night and also helped me telephone Bill. "I'll be right up" he said. But he didn't come until the next day. I expected him right away, but he said, "It's not just around the corner like it is in England." I loved New York. Just like London.

A few weeks later we were married in Jersey City, where Bill's sister lived. It was a Catholic wedding. We had to get married in the rectory, but people waited for us in the church. You know how you go to the zoo to see the panda? Well, they wanted to see this new creature that had just arrived. I met them all after the wedding; Italians, Greeks, Irish, and they were great. A nice cosmopolitan wedding.

I told Bill, "Now I'm going to be homesick." I didn't like this and that, but I never said it. I went home in 1946 and took our baby daughter with me. A British newspaper said I was the first GI bride to come back for a visit. Many of them were still waiting for a ship to go over! Norma came to America later, bringing nice family pieces on the boat with her.

I missed some of the English vegetables, especially marrow, until I saw some in a vegetable stand in Arlington, Virginia. "I'll have one of those marrows," I told the man. He looked puzzled and said "Show me where you see one and tell me what you do with it." I pointed to a lovely large green marrow and told him that we cut it up, cook it and serve it with a nice white sauce. "That's a watermelon," he replied and cut one in half to show me. I was shocked to see that it was blood-red inside and full of black pips, too. Since then I've grown some lovely marrow (a fine-grained squash the size of a melon) in my own garden. I'll never forget that little man with the vegetable stand. I hope he gets a good seat in heaven because of what I put him through.

My old man used to say when I cooked something, "Now my Aunt Frances (who raised Bill) used to do this and do that." Until one day I said, "Hey! You didn't marry your Aunt Frances; you married me, so you're going to eat what I cook and to hell with your Aunt Frances." Of course, when an American cook book said "put the meat and vegetables into a kettle," I was at a loss because I only boil water for tea in a kettle. Then I found out it meant a Dutch oven, a stock pot to me.

It was an adventure, a challenge coming here. I came to marry Bill; it wasn't to come to America. I could have lived my life without America and married some old Cockney. But now I've got my family and three grandsons here. Bill has retired from the Government, and we keep busy with our flower and vegetable garden, church, hobbies and a summer home on the Chesapeake Bay. My life is here, but my roots are not. Let's put it that way.

* * * * *

Pat as a civilian, Gilbert and Annie as members of the armed forces were among those who arrived in America during World War II and then stayed. They had married American citizens, and after tackling the official hurdles, they settled down in their new country. For most of the foreign GI spouses living abroad, however, it was not until after Hitler lost his war in Europe and the imperialistic Japanese finally surrendered to the Allies in September 1945 that legislative, social and transportation issues were addressed for those dependents to sail to America.

It would take an act of Congress to get things moving.

2

1946: UNITED STATES ARMY WAR BRIDES OPERATION

"I never heard of the purge!"

Invading armies had traditionally carried off with them the young women of the land they occupied. The Americans, doing things as usual on a grand scale, removed whole ship loads, the largest and certainly the most willing such contingent ever to leave the shores of Britain.

Norman Longmate, *The G.I,'s: The Americans in Britain 1942-1945*

Recently, when a young girl in England was asked what she thought of the World War II American soldiers taking home thousands of British brides, she looked surprised and said, "I heard about that war, but I never heard of the purge." Gasp! Actually, it was more the way Norman Longmate had rather humorously written when describing the exodus in his book. As for the GIs and their brides, they long remembered the stream of military and governmental redtapism that accompanied every step in their quest to be together.

The Second World War officially ended on 2 September 1945, VJ-Day, when General Yoshijiro Umezu, on behalf of the Japanese Imperial Government, signed the surrender documents dictated by the Allies aboard the *U.S.S. Missouri* in Tokyo Bay. In the chaotic months following this momentous day, there was an outcry by the war brides for ships to expedite getting them to the United States. While everyone agreed that first priority must be given to the homeward bound troops, the girls realized that it would take a struggle for them to get some action too.

"GI Bride Wallflowers" the cynics in Britain named the waiting wives. That did it! Nearly 1,000 women held a stormy meeting with Ambassador John G. Winant's special assistant, Commander Herbert Agar, at Caxton Hall in central London. A resolution asking for help was adopted and sent to a commission in the United States that was studying the problem.

Immigration laws in the U.S. were extremely restrictive at the time, and something had to be done. Members of Congress were being showered with appeals by GI constituents to act on legislation that would help get their wives into the U.S.A.

In Washington, D.C. the *War Brides Act* (Public Law 271, 79th Congress) was soon passed unanimously by both Houses of Congress and signed into law on 28 December 1945 by President Harry Truman. After passage, alien spouses of citizen members of the armed forces were officially "deemed to be nonquota immigrants" and would not need a visa. Application for admission to the country under this act had to be filed within three years of the date of its passage. After being "medically examined," these war brides could enter the United States as soon as transportation was available. But there were potent restrictions that caused dismay to some women.

> Under the terms of this law, a wife may file her own application for admission for herself and her children, but the application for government transportation MUST be filed by her husband. If the husband does not apply for government transportation or if he cancels his application, his wife cannot come to the United States unless she can afford to pay for commercial transportation.

Women's rights were practically "naught" then, or simply ignored. Commercial transportation was very expensive and practically impossible to obtain in those early postwar days, thereby taking away the wife's chance of seeking a possible reunion with her husband. Under the *War Brides Act* war widows, fiancées, wives of dishonorably discharged servicemen and illegitimate children were all ineligible for government sponsored transportation and "nonquota entry" into the country.

Back home in the United States, General Eisenhower was cornered by irate women representing the "Bring Back Daddy Association" and also by the "Fathers' Release Association" trying to get their men back home. The war was over, but postwar turmoil existed, and the General declared that "no one would be released earlier than their points called for." American wives of soldiers who stayed with the Army of Occupation in Germany pressured officials for ships or planes to Europe, so they could join their husbands **over there.**

Other American civilians grumbled that the GI brides would take up precious berths that should go instead to servicemen in Europe still waiting to sail home. In a 7 January 1946 letter, an Indiana constituent protested to Representative Louis Ludlow that the British brides should wait until all GIs had returned because his son had been waiting for ninety days at Le Havre for a ship. At the same time, Lieutenant-General Joseph L. Collins of the War Department in Washington, D.C. pointed out: "The shipment of these (GI bride) dependents will not be permitted to delay any soldier who would otherwise be ready to return."

Priority points had been established by the War Department a few days after VE-Day (8 May 1945). A total of eighty-five points meant that a soldier had qualified for immediate embarkation and honorable discharge in the States. This high-point figure was lowered proportionally each month thereafter. From a peak of nearly three million American servicemen in Britain during the war, by 1 November 1945, the number had dropped to 77,000. Most troops in the European Theater of Operation (ETO) had gone on to the Continent, and now that the war with Japan was over, would sail directly home from there.

Very soon after the Christmas 1945 passage of the *War Brides Act*, a conference was held in Washington, D.C. by representatives from the War Department, Public Health Service, Department of State, Justice Department, American Red Cross, Immigration and Naturalization Service, War Shipping Administration and several domestic and foreign steamship lines, and a coordinated plan of operation was drawn up.

Tagged the *War Brides Operation*, and *Operation Diaper,* it was characteristically treated by the Army just like a troop movement, though with some refinements. Assistance from the American Red Cross was requested since their brand of expertise would be especially valuable in this case. Trained personnel helped many young women and babies en route from railway stations, at the reception centers, transfer points and ports on both sides of the ocean. American Red Cross staff also served in various capacities aboard the bride ships.

The Army needed help in streamlining the processing of so many individuals for immigration. Subsequently, an official from the Department of Justice, Ernest E. Salisbury, sailed to England in January 1946 along with a team of twenty-five Immigration Officers. "The Army welcomed us with open arms and were very happy to turn over to us the immigration part of the processing," said Salisbury. Ship manifest forms were shortened and immigration red tape was slashed in half. Even so, each would-be traveler, used to bureaucratic ways, knew she would have to endure many stepping stones before arriving at the foot of a ship's gangplank for embarkation. After applying for travel, the preliminary steps were:

1. Questionnaire to be answered and returned to the U.S. Transportation Office in London.
2. British Passport required for identification only; not needed for entry into America if traveling under the 28 December 1945 act of Congress.
3. Smallpox vaccination certificate.
4. Letter of Authority to a bank--authorizing transfer of a limited amount of sterling into dollars.

Trouble simmered briefly at the Tidworth Staging Area when American military personnel protested that their return home to the States was being delayed. On 30 December 1945, they cabled President Truman with their complaints about being assigned to process the GI brides:

This work will be accomplished by American officers and men for **British Subjects** [wives of Americans] on a British post but this work could be handled more efficiently by British service groups. Majority of soldiers have more than two years service. We realize that this operation is delaying our return home.

Six years of war had sharply strained British resources, and many economic wartime restrictions, such as food and clothes rationing, remained in effect and continued for ten years afterward. The acute labor shortage and lack of ready manpower in Britain also threatened to slow things down.

After trying to pass the buck and make Britain responsible for processing the wives of GI servicemen, the U.S. Army obtained substitutes for the men stationed at Tidworth who had enough points for going home. Replacements were found with the "closeout" of the Wharton American Technical School and the Shrivenham American University, two army schools operating in England. They included not only officers and men from these schools but also some local British civilians. German and Italian prisoners-of-war were utilized as well, for various jobs performed under military supervision.

Slowly at first, on a trial-and-error basis, the consolidated effort of transporting the huge number of GI brides sharpened into positive action.

1946: THE BRIDES FLOTILLA

In the New Year of 1946, most of the GI brides were still waiting at home for ships to take them to America to be reunited with their husbands. Behind the scenes, meanwhile, the U.S. Army's *War Brides Operation* had geared into action, and a veritable fleet of troop and hospital ships was being converted to make them suitable for the brides, and fitted with nurseries for their babies. Each ship was staffed with Army medical personnel and skilled Red Cross workers. Wartime conditions still prevailed, and supplies were basically utilitarian, but the girls never expected anything approaching a luxury cruise. To them, the prospect of being able to buy ration-free clothing, sweets and food was something marvelous to look forward to. By the middle of January, the first ship was ready and waiting in Southampton for the war brides with the highest priority. Suddenly it was time to GO!

Some of the girls wore smart "Utility" labeled clothing--dresses, coats or the ever popular English suits. To save precious resources during the war, the British Government had introduced "Utility" designer clothes that used less material, were stylish and serviceable. All clothing was still strictly rationed, nonetheless--but sometimes available on "the black market" for outrageous prices.

The first official GI Bride ship departed on 26 January 1946 amid a blaze of publicity when the *Argentina* left England with 626 U.S. dependents aboard. It was soon followed by the *Queen Mary* carrying 2,340 passengers and an amazing flotilla of ships of all sizes sailing back and forth across the Atlantic between Southampton and New York City. Elsewhere, the first official brides' ship to sail from "down under" was on 19 February 1946 when the *Monterey* left Sydney carrying 815 Australian and New Zealand girls and babies. Also, by the end of February, a contingent of Italian war brides sailed to the United States on the *Algonquin*, and on 5 March the *Goethals* left Le Havre carrying 450 French, Belgian, Dutch and Luxembourg brides. Two days later, the first of three shiploads of brides from Northern Ireland sailed on the *Gibbons* from Belfast.

The ships used in the 1946 armada that sailed to America ranged in size from the small wartime American Liberty Ships, carrying 225 war brides and babies, to the two giant British "*Queens*" with up to 3,000 dependents aboard. The following ships sailed in the brides flotilla:

Algonquin	*John Ericsson*
Aquitania	*Larkspur*
Argentina	*Mauretania*
Brazil	*Mount Vernon*
Bridgeport	*President Tyler*
Cristobal	*Queen Elizabeth*
E. B. Alexander	*Queen Mary*
Fitzhugh Lee	*Santa Paula*
Goethals	*Saturnia*
Hamilton	*Thomas H. Barry*
Henry Gibbons	*Vulcania*
Holbrook	*Wakefield*
Huddleston	*Washington*
James Parker	*Zebulon B. Vance*

The GI Bride ships that sailed from Australia and New Zealand to America carried up to 1,200 passengers each:

Fred C. Ainsworth	*Mariposa*
Lurline	*Monterey*
Marine Phoenix	*Orion*

ACROSS THE OCEANS, FULL STEAM AHEAD!

GOOD-BYE, WHITE CLIFFS OF DOVER

*It was my turn to board the giant ship. With
youthful optimism and confidence born of
love, I climbed aboard, leaving my dear
familiar world behind.*

30 March 1946

That is how I felt on a lovely springlike day when embarking on the *Queen Mary*, one of the bride ships bound from Southampton to New York. How lucky and how exciting to be among the thousands aboard such a superb liner. Married just a few months, I was amazed that the U.S. Army Transportation Office had squeezed me in so soon, but the time was ripe for action, and there I was.

Not until much later did I suddenly remember my mother's sad face when the large buff envelope had arrived containing my travel orders. Then, in another moment, she smiled and simply said that she would miss me. It would be ten years before I could return home to England for a visit. By then I had become a mother myself and better understood her unspoken concern and anxiety for her daughter going off to a faraway land. I had also learned what the pangs of homesickness and sudden feelings of isolation felt like.

Every foreign war bride (or groom) and minor child of citizen members of the United States armed forces was eligible for free government transportation to America after the GI spouse applied for it. The *Military Appropriation Act*, Fiscal Year 1946, contained a provision which provided for their sea and land transportation at government expense. According to a few letters received by members of Congress, taxpayers were angry to be footing this bill. One woman said she believed there was a slogan in Britain, "Nab a Yank, and go to America free," and consequently the girls would soon be pouring into the country on every boat. She did not know of **anyone** (her emphasis) who was not thoroughly disgusted and indignant.

The whole operation became the joint responsibility of the U.S. Department of State and the Army. The war brides traveled together, and all had similar accommodations, regardless of their husbands' military or naval rank. Top priority went to the dependents of those servicemen who had already returned stateside. Early in January 1946, the official *War Brides Operation* began, and the first group of GI brides received their long-awaited travel orders:

> Under provisions of War Department Circular 245, dated 11 August 1945, the following dependent(s) of U.S. Servicemen are, subject to passport and diplomatic clearance, authorized and invited to proceed from points in the United Kingdom to destinations in the United States.

There were conditions: "Do not travel if you are over six months pregnant, or you have a baby under six weeks of age, or your child is ill." A special telegram form was enclosed, to be used if unable to travel, for whatever reason. For those who qualified and were able to go, there were instructions for the initial leg of their transatlantic journey and orders to bring:

1. Marriage & birth certificates. Children born of an American citizen need Form No.240, Consular Report of Birth.
2. British ration book & clothing coupon book.
3. National Identity Card (to be collected by British authorities).
4. Form I-136 (preliminary application form for admission to the United States) and two passport photos.
5. Luggage (up to 200 lbs & 50 lbs for each child).

A tan-colored cardboard label was included with the travel orders: "Kindly tie this label to your coat so that it will be prominently displayed." Thus equipped, the intrepid voyagers set out from familiar home and hearth for an unknown life with their "Yankee" husbands awaiting them across the sea. The first stop was the railway station to catch a train that would take them south to Tidworth or Bournemouth.

London's Waterloo Station was the main train terminal used for the departing GI brides, about a third of whom had children. Special trains with American Red Cross workers aboard traveled with the group on a two-hour journey to the staging areas. It was so crowded on the station platforms with girls and their babies that the "parade of perambulators, strollers and carry-cots" was compared to the much earlier evacuation of children from the London Blitz. Now it was grandparents who were left behind weeping as the final whistle blew, the smoky steam-engine started to move, and the train chugged out of the station. Out of their lives. They wondered if they would ever see their daughters and grandchildren again. From Waterloo station the special trains took the brides to one of two U.S. Army reception centers: Perham Down Camp, Tidworth, Wiltshire on Salisbury Plain and not far from prehistoric Stonehenge; or The Carlton Hotel, a grand seaside hotel in Bournemouth, Hampshire, where the Gulf Stream nurtures splendid palm trees. Women with small babies generally went to the latter where about 500 mothers and infants could be accommodated at one time. Tidworth's capacity totaled 4,000 GI dependents.

The girls had Army Post Exchange (PX) privileges, so they could get ration-free treats, like sweets, cigarettes and toilet articles. Their luggage was inspected to see that they carried no "war souvenirs or fire-arms!" Those not recently vaccinated for smallpox had to be inoculated. The food was typical U.S. Army fare, much more abundant and different from what the girls were used to. It was dished out onto Army "plates" by German prisoners-of-war, cafeteria style, and usually tasted good, except for a few strange items such as sweet potatoes. And corn! The girls thought that only farm animals ate that stuff (known to them as maize).

By fulfilling U.S. immigration requirements before sailing, the war brides would bypass the infamous Ellis Island complex for aliens when they reached New York City. The stories and indignities sustained by earlier, oftentimes "steerage", emigrants at Ellis Island, the Isle of Tears, were well-known to many Europeans at that time.

Processing by the U.S. Army in England took an average of five days. In mid-1946, Ernest E. Salisbury, the man sent by the Department of Justice to oversee the immigration process, wrote a firsthand description of what happened at Tidworth:

SALISBURY:
Groups of 25 brides entered with their filled out Forms I-136. Clerks then typed Forms I-135 and AR-4 (the fingerprint card) from the information on I-136 and stapled on the photographs. With the I-135, I-136 and AR-4 in her possession the bride passed along to the medical doctor who examined her (nose, throat and skin inspection) and stamped the I-136, if found admissible.

The bride, with her documents, then passed along and had her fingerprints taken on the reverse of AR-4. At this stage, an officer lifted the AR-4, I-135 and I-136 and checked the name of the bride (and any children) on the Manifest Form I-417 which had been prepared in advance from the Army Passenger List. The bride then passed along to the agent of the steamship company who issued tickets and collected the required Head Tax of two pounds sterling.

Last in the processing line was the British Immigration Officer who checked on the bride's permission to leave England and collected her ration book, clothing book and national identity card.

Seemingly stripped of their former identity, the girls faced the most solemn moment in the process. Many girls, however, were too excited to ponder their in-between national status. Time for that later. They only knew that in their hearts love was calling. But most girls would undergo a slow metamorphosis of sorts before coming to terms with their new identity and life in another land.

After the U.S. Army processing was completed, the GI brides were finally taken from the reception center by special train or bus to Southampton docks, where their ship lay waiting. Southampton was one of the ancient English ports from whence the seventeenth-century Pilgrims had sailed when going to a new life in America. Now these modern Pilgrim brides, leaving Britain, would follow suit. Linked together in a shared venture, the girls, be it Pamela, Jill, Iris, Daphne, felt a common bond with one another. As their ship pulled away from Southampton's busy pier, they watched quietly, and most of them had tears gently rolling down their cheeks.

Not all the women sustained the courage to go. At the last moment a few clung to the railing of the gangplank and then got off. One woman, with a son, was already so homesick that she could not bear to leave and live so far away from her family. She stayed, and her GI husband later joined her in England.

On 26 January 1946 the first designated bride ship, the *Argentina*, sailed for New York City with 626 dependents aboard, including one "male war bride" who was married to an American servicewoman. British newspapers and newsreel cameras recorded the departure, seeing it in contemporary terms as the "greatest human interest story since D-Day." Shared feelings of goodwill for their departing pilgrim-daughters were exemplified by the Mayor and Mayoress of Southampton who were on the dock and wished them GODSPEED!

Ironically, as their America-bound ship sailed out of port, the girls heard jeers and shouts of "You'll be sorry!" and "You bloody twerps!" or worse from British warriors who crowded the decks of their incoming troopship. They were among the six million British men who had served world-wide during the Second World War. After spending years of fighting overseas, they now showed their disdain for those girls whom the "Yanks had pinched."

Oh! Those Forms at Tidworth

Sailing o'er the ocean wide
This happy band of "GI Brides"
Yes! at last! we're on our way
Bound for that land--the U.S.A.
*But oh! those **forms** we had to fill*
Have we more to fill in still?
You know my height, my weight in pounds
That I've hazel eyes, and my hair is brown
You know I'm British through and through
Married when single? Yes! that is true
You have my photos--two or three
Plus finger prints taken. Oh! poor me
My place of birth and date when born
*Oh! please, **say that's the last of forms***
'Cause Sir, had Colombus with same had been bothered
I'm afraid that the States would still be undiscovered

Penned by Hazel Raeburn Garrison

16 April 1946: "Rae" finally left Tidworth, boarded the *Queen Mary* and five days later was reunited with her husband, Cecil, in New York.

HELLO, NEW WORLD

Debarkation Plans for Mrs. GI Joe

The lucky girls will be met by their husbands in New York City but don't worry because travel plans for the rest of the girls have been made and include train reservations, tickets, transfers en route and luggage, both hold and hand. Remember, the Army will not send you to a destination unless it has been verified that "That Man" is there waiting. In short, **consider yourself parcel post delivery, so relax!**

Mrs. GI Joe newspaper, American Red Cross,
aboard the *Queen Mary*, 4 April 1946.

"Gonna Take a Sentimental Journey!" Nine days at sea, long after their familiar English shores had slipped from view, the first official shipload of GI brides sailing aboard the *Argentina*, glimpsed the outline of America on the far horizon. "I felt a sense of relief and much excitement to see land," remembers one girl after the tempestuous ocean crossing. "Rather like a Columbus or Sir Walter Raleigh discovering a distant and unknown land." They passed the Statue of Liberty. Now there was no more time to loiter and daydream on the deck. Even the rough voyage and winter's bitterly cold weather was forgotten in a final frenzy of activity aboard the crowded ship in preparation for going ashore. It had been a year or more since most of the girls had seen their husbands, and all thoughts now turned to their longed-for romantic reunion, so close at hand.

The brides were organized into groups for going ashore. New labels, color-coded this time, were to be worn to indicate their final destination in the States. Husbands had already been contacted by the American Red Cross Home Service Department, but only those men living on the East Coast were expected or allowed to meet their wives in New York City. Those brides going to distant regions of the vast United States were to be transported overland by train and then by bus, if necessary, to reach their final destination. Army and Red Cross personnel shepherded those brides from the ship to train stations where they were given tickets and seen safely aboard the right train. The Red Cross had already informed the girls that it would cost them about $5 per day, plus $3 for children, for train meals. But, the ARC was "at your side," in case of fund shortage or any other personal problem.

First to leave the ship were the war brides being met in New York City. Some anxious husbands had arrived in town a day or two before the *Argentina* docked. The variables of ocean travel were such that the hour (or day!) a ship would arrive was uncertain. Also, progress had been slowed down by the frigid winter's ice-floes on the Hudson River and by a last-minute tugboat strike. On 4 February 1946, despite these added difficulties, the ship was finally moored at Pier 54. GI husbands meeting the *Argentina* had to wait at the Red Cross Chapter house across town on Lexington Avenue to greet their wives. In the near future, however, reunions would take place right on the pier. Then, as one of those brides recollected:

> We had to wait until we were called. Then we were allowed to go down the gangplank and as we did, we handed in our name and then they called out our husband's name. And there he was. It was thrilling!

Amid the ecstatic hugs, kisses and feelings of exhilaration, perhaps the greatest initial shock was seeing their previously uniform-clad Yanks now wearing civvies (civilian clothes) and looking even stranger in an Al Capone style broad-brimmed hat. For better or for worse, they had safely reached the New World.

"It was an arrival the like of which New York had never before experienced," wrote one of the 200 reporters who were present that day to interview the new "colonists" from England. Mayor William O'Dwyer welcomed the newcomers, band music blared, and the brides waited eagerly to set forth. The bright dabs of color on shore sent shock waves through the girls as they took in the scene. After being accustomed to six years of strict and austere "making do," the black-out and bleak dark bombed-out buildings, the contrast of New York City's blaring gaiety and colorful vibrancy, as yellow and checkered taxi cabs dodged around the streets, quite took their breath away.

American news coverage of the arrival of those first GI brides was just as complete as the British reporting of their departure had been. Reporters rushed to describe this "Anglo-American love story, multiplied many times over" with the happy endings they had witnessed that day, and the start of a new beginning. Most of the husbands, all across the country, still waited expectantly for their brides to arrive by train or bus.

Hometown newspapers ran stories about GI brides arriving in their areas. Major newspapers, newsreel films and magazines concentrated on the first official sailings: the *Argentina* and then the *Queen Mary*, which arrived a few days later. Thus the *War Brides Operation* had been successfully launched, and for months thereafter there would be scores of transatlantic (and Pacific) crossings bringing tens-of-thousands of brides and children to the United States. The bustle and activity from Europe during one month, March 1946 for example, involved sixteen British bride ships sailing from Southampton and five ships with Continental brides from the French port of Le Havre. Also in March, a group of Italian brides sailed from Naples, and 127 Scandinavian war brides got underway from Oslo, Norway.

According to an unclassified Army history record dated 11 May 1948, *War Brides and Their Shipment to the United States*, the only serious incidents of the entire operation involved the *Zebulon Vance* and the *Santa Paula*, both sailing from Le Havre. Dependents bound on a train for the latter ship had been exposed to a civilian suffering from spinal meningitis and had to be isolated to prevent spreading the disease. Fortunately, no further developments were observed, and all dependents later sailed on the *Henry Gibbons*.

The other "serious incident(s)" mentioned in the Army report had more tragic consequences. During the 7 May 1946 voyage of the Liberty Ship, *Zebulon Vance*, three babies sickened and died from an infectious type of diarrhea (or cholera infantum). Another five babies perished after arriving in New York. Then in June several more of the babies died, taking a toll of thirteen out of the fifty-seven children who had sailed together. Evidently some of the infants had been ill with diarrhea at the *Camp Philip Morris* processing center before boarding the ship at Le Havre, but the Port Surgeon had given them a "clean bill of health."

Naturally, the death of those babies raised adverse publicity. It was reported on 6 June 1946 in the *New York Times* that an Army Board of Inquiry "blamed Dutch, Belgian, French and Polish brides for improper hygiene practiced by these mothers despite the advice of attending nurses." Three of the brides testified to the extremely cramped and dirty conditions on board ship and complained about the rudeness of some of the Army personnel. One French bride was upset because she said it took her two days to persuade a ship's physician to take her baby's temperature, and a Belgian wife said she lined up several times with her sick two-year old son to see a doctor but never reached him.

Dr. Henry M. Friedman of the U.S. Public Health Service testified that he found food thrown under the bunks of the *Zebulon Vance* and that "scabies, lice and tuberculosis were being found among some war brides" arriving. There were bound to be some careless "bedraggled" girls as well as some "flashy" women among the thousands who came over, but the saying, "like attracted like" seemed to be proven in many cases by the kind of men they had married.

Tidworth's Perham Down processing center also came under attack, 27 May 1946, when a Los Angeles GI veteran compared it to what he called a concentration-type camp after his wife had been there. He said his baby son became ill on the voyage to America aboard the *Queen Mary,* and blamed "the British camp" for the deaths of nine babies from a mysterious illness as they arrived in New York. This allegation was denied by the U.S. Army Transportation Corp.

After the War Department completed its *Vance Board of Inquiry,* which investigated every phase of the epidemic and its sorrowful aftermath, the Army was cleared of any "negligence and culpability," but it was recommended that more stringent regulations be enforced. After 10 June 1946, no baby under six months of age was permitted to travel. (The minimum age had originally been six weeks and later changed to three months). Also, the "load percentage of each vessel" was restricted to 25% of children under six-years of age. No woman over six months pregnant could travel. These restrictions delayed the reunions of many families, but it was better than "rushing the operation regardless of health risks."

So the U.S. Army's *War Brides Operation* continued unabated, although changing its policy as needed. American Red Cross officials had noted earlier in 1946 that the army was beginning to discover that the war brides could not be "treated as GIs, nor as crates of oranges" but had to be looked after as dependents of servicemen.

As the U.S. Army got more adept at handling the movement of thousands of GI dependents from overseas, the number of travelers decreased. The peak had been reached by early summer and the official "sentimental journeys" ended not many months later. By the end of 1946 the Tidworth U.S. Army processing center was closed, and the last special bride ship had sailed from Southampton. However, the U.S. Army in England continued to process the requests of thousands of war brides who were still applying to travel, and they sailed from Southampton on a more individualized basis.

On the Continent, the Allied armies of occupation in Germany had settled down, and by August 1946 the U.S. Army had transferred its major Continental port facilities and staging area for GI brides from Le Havre to Bremerhaven. The War Department reiterated that war brides who had permission to travel could obtain their own commercial transportation, and hundreds of war brides did just that. They could apply for a limited reimbursement of their fares later on.

According to contemporary articles in American newspapers and magazines, the arrival of the GI brides was viewed with great interest and warmth. In January and February 1946 *Newsweek* and *Life* magazines highlighted GI bride stories and photographs. Sunday paper magazine-supplements printed human interest articles telling how the new pioneers were settling down. But when articles appeared with public-baiting statements like "American servicemen consider British girls better wives than American girls," it was bound to touch a nerve and produce negative reactions. Great for circulation!

The Ladies Home Journal joined in the fray by printing the complaints of an American wife whose husband had served in Europe: "My husband says the girls in Europe are more human and understanding than we are." A letter from an American lady which appeared in the 10 March 1946 *New York Times* defended the British brides, saying they have "better manners and more profound sincerity" while the girls back home only thought about nylon stockings, movie heroes and the latest gadgets. Though she believed American women were much better looking than their British counterparts, she concluded that they should take stock of themselves.

In Washington, D.C. members of Congress continued to receive letters from unhappy constituents. Senator Theodore F. Green received a long letter dated 23 February 1946 from a lady in his home state of Rhode Island. She was upset enough to write because she was afraid the country was being over-run "with the dregs of Europe and Asia . . . by women who **hi-jack** our boys in a weak moment" and that the "very foundations of our land, our homes and our Treasury are at stake." Senator Green merely informed his constituent that transportation for all dependents of U.S. servicemen, including alien wives and children of those who had served overseas, was provided for under the *Military Appropriation Act*, Fiscal Year 1946 (Public Law 126, 79th Congress).

In a more optimistic light, Ernest E. Salisbury, the Department of Justice official now back in the U.S.A. from Europe, predicted that the brides who came over in the mass migration were eager to start a new life in America and that they "would make real contributions" to the social and economic progress of the nation.

What a field day Talk Show hosts would have had discussing the pros-and-cons of the alien war brides streaming into the land, if such programs had been popular in 1946. But the upbeat mission of people at the time was to sort out their own postwar lives, loves and jobs, leaving no time for endless chatter shows as entertainment.

Except for occasional bursts of publicity later on, the newcomers vanished into the flow of American life. Because the British brides spoke the same language (except for a few curiously different expressions and meanings) and shared similar cultural and religious backgrounds, they soon adapted to their new homes. It was a good start. At the same time they shared the reservations and feelings of all first-generation immigrants when it came to being completely assimilated into the life and soul of another land. It was not easy. Their place of birth and old home would always be close to their hearts.

Homesickness and loneliness were common problems, and some bits of prejudice did not help. On one of her visits to England, Mrs. Eleanor Roosevelt had addressed a gathering of 1,000 GI brides at Rainbow Corner, an American Red Cross Club in the heart of London, and gave them many pointers about life in America. As she listed her 12-item guide to the U.S.A. she warned the girls to be "patient with our women" and to be prepared for some "unreasoning prejudice."

Like the aggravated homeward-bound British Tommies (who had pre-viously complained that the Yanks were "oversexed, overpaid and over here"), some American girls were equally vexed with the war brides. They yelled "Go back to England" said one bride who arrived in New York, 28 June 1946 on the *E.B.Alexander*. Another bride recalled that she met some married women who seemed resentful that I "had caught" one of their boys. Perhaps the 2,000 girls who married black soldiers had the hardest time of all in America. They encountered racial discrimination from all sorts of people, including African-Americans. Suffering despair and isolation, some went back to England. "No one back there to even have a cup of tea with!"

Divorces were not as numerous as the pessimists had predicted. According to a report by Elizabeth Valentine, ninety percent of the foreign GI brides "knew their husbands longer before marrying than did the American girls" who married during the war. Their marriages also enjoyed a higher success rate, perhaps because divorce was frowned upon by most foreign women at this time, and also their options in a strange country were more limited. They stuck it out. Looking back, one girl remembered the hard and lonely adjustments she had to make, and then humorously added that "he only wanted to keep me bare-foot and pregnant!"

Vivien Harris, writing in the *Red Cross Courier*, May 1946, quoted several reasons for early divorce, all from the man's point of view. "His wife would not join him in the United States." "He wanted to forget about the marriage." "He was still fond of his wife but he yielded to family pressure who wanted him to divorce his foreign wife." There was little, if any, financial support sent to the wife and children in cases like these. Family allowances stopped following the discharge of the GI and the husband's contribution was a voluntary matter. The ARC helped where it could and also assisted the wife in obtaining her legal rights. Often a hopeless cause.

Unless a castoff GI bride still living overseas had enough money of her own to provide transportation to the States and could guarantee not to become a "public charge" once there, she could not contest the divorce or hope for a reconciliation. If a divorce was inevitable, her presence might have resulted in a court order for support. Divorce problems and lack of child support caused much heartache to the unwanted war bride. It was soon realized that there was a "callous disregard" for the rights of war brides left abroad and this did a "great deal of injury, especially to British women" who had married GIs in greater numbers than those living in the other fifty countries or territories where Americans had been stationed. The British government tried to help with these problems but because each state had its own divorce laws it was difficult to come up with comprehensive legal help for the girl still living outside the U.S.A.

Fortunately, most girls who did come to America adjusted to all cultural shock challenges and loneliness so their marriages endured. The marriages that eventually failed, did so for personal factors that would have applied anywhere.

American public interest in the GI brides lasted only while their 1946 oceanic crossings made the headlines. American Red Cross Home Service personnel, nevertheless, continued to help the U.S. Army in expediting the transportation of GI brides until the 28 December 1948 deadline when Public Law 271, the *War Brides Act,* expired. The Army was "well pleased with the efficient manner" in which ARC workers had assisted them while the official war bride project was in effect.

In a similar vein, J. Harrison Heckman, Executive Director of the ARC New York Chapter during this hectic period, wrote that the aid their 150-member staff and volunteers provided to the often bewildered war brides and their babies who came through the Port of New York was one of the "finest operations I have ever seen." This was accomplished, he said, even though the Chapter House seemed like a Bedlam of women and kids for many months!

Back home in the British Isles, where parents and siblings in particular missed their loved ones, the stories and publicity about the GI brides continued to crop up in the media. Not all coverage was favorable. Some journalists relished printing stories that gave the war brides "a bad name," or wrote about the inevitable hardships and loneliness that some of the girls suffered.

Nevertheless, in contrast to the global human misery and ruin cast on millions during the most extensive war mankind had ever experienced, the drama of the surviving GIs and their brides from overseas was a jubilant and creative phenomenon. Together, these couples had shared the danger of air raids, buzz bombs and other life threatening experiences, and the bonds thus created remained very meaningful throughout their married lives. **"Their marriages seem to be forged in steel,"** said Lynn Sherr of ABC News 20/20.

3

GI BRIDES LOOK BACK

*Reminiscences make one feel
so deliciously aged and sad.*

George Bernard Shaw, *Heartbreak House*

Certainly the ladies whose personal accounts ensue are fortunate because now, decades later, they can look back and remember their unique experiences as World War II pilgrim brides who sailed to America at war's end. Studying school books, reading about the New World or watching any of Hollywood's tinsel versions of American life "at the pictures" was scant preparation for the real thing, they soon discovered. Amazingly, many husbands had neglected to tell their brides very much about what day-to-day life back home was really like. No doubt they talked about their families, where they lived, their occupation and general things like that, but time was precious, so paramount in their relationship had been their blossoming love and concerns about the fates of war. Dreams of a future life together were all they had. Dreams were enough.

In 1945 the British *Good Housekeeping* magazine, in conjunction with the U.S. Office of War Information, tried to help by printing a *Bride's Guide to the U.S.A.* which offered bits of advice, information and statistics of various kinds. A glossary of **English**/American terms to study was added: **dustbin**/trash can; **face flannel**/wash cloth; **ladder**/run (in ladies' stockings); **biscuit**/cookie; **scone**/biscuit and **tramp**/bum!--slang and not a "nice" word in England at the time. The *Guide* advised the girls to "use the American names and pronunciation so as not to be misunderstood." At the same time, it advised them to keep their "charming accent" while they could.

Several articles in British newspapers warned the GI brides that life could be difficult for them because the "United States is not Utopia" and that perhaps many would have to face married life squeezed in with strange in-laws, or living in wooded rural backwaters where conditions were extremely primitive. Some of the more dire predictions proved true, but they stuck it out, remembering the old adage: "You made your bed, now lie on it!"

Other writers simply wished them good luck as they sailed off. Most importantly, with loving hearts and understanding husbands at their sides, most brides coped very well when they arrived in their fresh and strange environment.

TBPA: TRANSATLANTIC BRIDES & PARENTS ASSOCIATION

High Teas

Several fellow GI brides shared their reminiscences with me, and I have added my own. We are members of the *High Teas*, the esoteric name coined for the Vienna, Virginia branch of the TBPA, an Anglo-American society. Founded in 1946 in Great Britain by the parents of British girls who had married American and Canadian servicemen during the war, the association was able to charter planes so that parents and the war brides could afford to fly across the Atlantic to visit one another. Otherwise it would have cost "pots and pots of money." Today, the association remains primarily as a permanent link with our British heritage and provides fellowship, help and information on a local and national level. Social clubs such as this have become more meaningful and important to us as the years pass by. Through them we share a kinship that goes back a long way. Back to the land of our birth and young womanhood.

All of us whose narratives appear in this book are "original" GI brides (or grooms), having met our future spouses during the fateful years of World War II. Some couples were married while the war was being fought; others wed after hostilities ceased. The ensuing accounts, like variations on the theme of a heartfelt love-song, are of experiences shared by all of the brides who sailed to North America at that time.

Among those sailing across the ocean in the 1946 Brides Flotilla were five girls, Margaret, Eunice, Doris, Joan and Vera, who met when the *High Teas* was organized. They hailed from the London area, Luton, Newport and Weston-super-Mare. Another Londoner, Eileen, spent twenty-one years with her U.S. Army husband in postwar Germany before coming to live in the States, and later joining the club. They recall their adventures with mixed happy and sad emotions, much as they had felt back then.

London 1944: Margaret and Robert Garman

Margaret Willis from Richmond, Surrey, was educated in a convent and later worked as a bookkeeper for the Middlesex County Council in London. Sadly, her mother had died early in the war when Margaret was only fifteen years old. Her father relied on her to help raise her younger siblings until she left home.

Margaret has retained a firm and clear Mary-Poppins-type English accent and personality.

MARGARET:

My girlfriend, Rose, was always looking for an excuse to visit her aunt and uncle in Bury St. Edmonds, Suffolk. A lot of Americans were stationed there and Rose was "crazy" about Yanks. I must have been a proper goody-two-shoes because Rose's mother insisted that I go along with Rose the next time. That's where I met Bob Garman who was with the U.S. Army 8th Air Force. When Uncle John went for his usual pint of ale at the local pub, we went along, and Bob was one of several servicemen there.

I had not met any Americans before. My father was very strict and when he found out I was dating a Yank he went up like a balloon. He was angry and said many unkind things, warning me not to marry Bob. That bothered me--it has always bothered me. But Rose was the one who married the Englishman, and I married the Yank.

I came home from work one day and there was a telegram for me, and that was something big in those days. It was from Bob, saying, "I love you, I love you, I love you." Bob gave me an engagement ring, a small diamond (chuckles) and I wanted a knuckle-duster. We dated a long time, it wasn't a "hole in the corner" affair, and on 2 September 1944, we were married. My father was very unhappy that I had married against his wishes, and he was never reconciled to my marriage. He never came to see me. Bob and I were able to be together for several months before he was sent to the Continent. Carol was born late in 1945.

I had strong feelings about being British. America didn't seem real to me. Bob did say he would be "demobbed" in England but the U.S. Army had other ideas. He had to return to the States, and he had a job to go back to in Pennsylvania and "whither thou goest," so I followed. That's how we were raised in those days. My travel orders came in mid-March 1946, when Carol was three months old. I have four sisters and two brothers, but I didn't notify anyone that I was leaving, because of my father's attitude.

We went to the Tidworth Processing Camp. I felt humiliated and embarrassed when required to appear before a male doctor with just a robe on. I had only ever been to a lady doctor. When finally we left Tidworth for Southampton, girls were crying. None of us realized what we were getting into. Looking back, I don't think I was really as mature as I thought I was. It was such a final thing in those days.

> She said to me "anyone who has to have a bath
> every day has to be pretty damn dirty."

On 24 March 1946 I left on the *Brazil*, a converted prisoner-of-war ship sailing out of Le Havre and stopping for us in Southampton. When I got on board I found I was in the company of some prostitutes. I was a regular Carry Nation. Well, I was ashamed of some of the girls. The ship was not clean, the weather was rough, and it was a terrible journey. The babies had diarrhea from a much richer formula than they were used to--like Cow and Gate baby milk at home.

I volunteered to help the American Red Cross in the nursery where our babies usually stayed. We fed them, washed and cared for them. Most of the girls helped and took care of their babies, but one girl who consistently neglected her little boy was usually with the Captain. Well, she's not in there playing tiddlywinks, is she? I got on the Public Address system during one terrible storm, and called the mother to come and take care of her child. I thought the Captain was going to sling me overboard when I saw him on deck later on!

At last we passed the Statue of Liberty. When the ship docked, we saw the people in bright colors--at least they seemed brilliant after the lack of color during the war. We didn't realize how "dull" England was until we saw America. I had boasted that Bob would be the first one there, but he was late. Of course, some girls were not claimed, if that's the right word. When Bob finally arrived, he was wearing a hat with a huge brim. I wondered what he did with it when his ears got tired.

Bob took us to his hometown, Clearfield, Pennsylvania. His mother had a rented house which we had to buy. It had a coal stove with a "reservoir" that heated water. Upstairs there was a bathroom complete with fixtures but no running water. I would heat water to bathe Carol in the kitchen and then do the laundry. Later I carried buckets of water upstairs to the bathtub to take a bath. My mother-in-law was not supportive. She said to me "anyone who has to have a bath every day has to be pretty damn dirty." And to wash the child every day . . . well! The food was different. I longed for roast beef and Yorkshire pudding. I was homesick, lost weight, became ill and went down to 85 pounds.

"My mother came over on the Mayflower"

Fortunately, Bob's job sent him to another state. It was better when we moved and were happier on our own. We worked hard and gave our six children top priority. My son, Bobby, told his teacher, "My mother came over on the Mayflower." She laughingly told me this later on and suggested that I set him straight! I always volunteered to help in any school activity and taught at Sunday School. We were raised not to be vain or boastful, but I think that the things that make a staunch British person also make a damn good Yankee.

Bob died of cancer many years ago. I had to go to work full-time and made a successful business career for myself until my retirement. I think our children have grown up to be fine American citizens. One is a member of an elite group of U.S. Army musicians who play at inaugurations and state affairs at the White House. I'm proud of all of my children and grandchildren.

*   *   *   *   *

After nearly forty years, Margaret finally returned to England to attend a niece's wedding and she renewed ties with relatives there. It was a breakthrough. Now members of her family come here for visits and re-unions on American soil. Margaret's father had died, so they never did see one another again.

.

Donald and Eunice Upchurch
1944: St. Mary's Church, Luton

"Something borrowed"
Eunice is wearing her neighbor's wedding dress.

During the war, Eunice Isaac lived at home with her mother in Luton, Bedfordshire, and she was working for the British Home Stores in town when she met Don Upchurch. Eunice speaks with a soft attractive voice and in a confident manner.

EUNICE:

It was Wednesday, early closing, and my girlfriend and I had left work and paused to look at the daily war pictures and news displayed in the window of the newspaper office. Suddenly, a coin rolled by and stopped at my feet. When I looked up, I saw Don and his buddy. I returned the coin, and they introduced themselves. Don said "There's a fair in Bedford. Care to come to the fair?" That's how it started--but I have never come to terms with the coin rolling by. And Don's not talking!

Don was in the U.S. Army 8th Air Force stationed at Chicksands, Thurleigh, near Bedford. My mother liked Don very much from the start. Both my brothers were away in the Royal Engineers, and he was like a son to her. We became engaged on the 4th of July 1944 and were married four months later, 1st November, just before my eighteenth birthday.

At the close of the war, Don had a flight to Gibraltar, and he brought back a huge bunch of bananas for us. We took a photograph of them and put the picture in the window for the children to see. Some of them had never seen a banana--or remembered them from prewar days!

I had corresponded with Don's family in the States. Don was very straightforward with me and told me what his family situation was, what his life was like. I wasn't looking for Hollywood. I expected to be a housewife and a mother.

Carole was born on Boxing Day, 26 December 1945, and I had to wait until she was three months old before applying for transportation to America. I was anxious to get going, but it was extremely difficult leaving my mother (a widow). My eldest brother had been killed a few days after the D-Day landings and now I was going to live overseas. It was hard. In April 1946 I received my U.S. travel orders to go to Bournemouth for processing. My mother and sister-in-law came to London to see us leave on the train. Carole and I stayed ten days at the Carlton Hotel in Bournemouth. There were three girls and three babies assigned to our room, but we got out and enjoyed the beautiful sandy beach as often as we could. We sailed on the *E. B. Alexander* and were put into a huge cabin, thirty of us, and we slept three bunks high. The babies were in a nursery next door, watched by two army nurses, but we did all the work.

| I was told I "spoke good English for a foreigner." |

Conditions on the ship were not good overall. There was a lot of sickness aboard; also we got lice and had to tackle that problem. A few of the girls flirted with the crew and neglected their babies. The best part was toward the end of the voyage when we put on a Variety Show. I danced in the chorus and sang "Wanting You" from "New Moon." One of the brides was a London show girl, and she choreographed the whole show. It was fun.

We reached New York, 6 May 1946, after twelve days at sea. Don was told to wait for us in Illinois. We were sent there by train, and it took two more days. An army lieutenant was assigned to take us to the station, but on the way one of the heels on my shoes broke! We stopped at a shoe shop, and I rushed in and bought TWO pairs of shoes--a red pair and a white pair with high-heels, platform soles, brass-studded and toe-less. As unlike the rationed British wartime austerity shoes as possible!

I had a good reception when I arrived at Don's house in Carterville. Don's family had ten acres of land, and he had lived all his life on a farm. We moved into a very basic house. It was square, divided into four rooms with a doorway between each room so you could go round and round. No closet, no bathroom, no running water, just an outdoor toilet. Don used to go to the gas station and fill up huge bottles with town water for drinking and cooking. We had a well, and I used a long cylinder type thing to draw water for my laundry. We had a gas stove, and I had to heat a big old wash tub on top of the stove for my laundry water and our bath water. Having been raised in a city, the lack of indoor plumbing was a challenging experience for me.

I got a job, and Don's mother looked after Carole while I worked. This was a temporary situation because Don had gone back to college to get his degree. I took a correspondence course before I became a citizen. Earlier someone had asked me if I had "civilization" papers yet. Southern Illinois was a farming and coal mining area, and some of the people there were not well educated. I was taken aback when I was told I "spoke good English for a foreigner."

I was very shy and quiet, and I was asked by people to "say something" so they could hear my accent. However, I tried to stifle my English accent when our three daughters were young because I didn't want to confuse them. Still, they are well-versed in Christopher Robin stories, British holidays and traditions. Now, we have eight grandchildren and one great-grandchild. We like to take them, after graduating from high school, on a special trip to England. We were proud when our eldest grandson, a U.S. Marine, served in the Gulf War.

* * * * *

Eunice and Don visited England many times, but their most memorable visit was in 1984, to celebrate their 40th wedding anniversary. Through a local newspaper and the BBC program, *London Plus,* Eunice traced her bridesmaids and publicized the occasion so that long-lost friends were able to rejoin the bride and groom as they renewed their marriage vows at a special Marriage Thanksgiving Service performed at St. Mary's Church in Luton, where they had first been married. "I wanted to relive the biggest step I made in my life," said Eunice. Sadly, nine years later Don died of cancer.

Doris in Beechwood Park, Newport, Wales

Barrage balloon in the background.

Doris Norley spent the war years living in Newport and working at the main post office as a telegraphist. She joined a brigade of Women Fire-fighters at work and learned how to use the big hoses in case of fire on the premises during air raids. The dock areas of nearby Cardiff and Bristol were prime targets and heavily bombed by German planes.

Doris was amongst those who volunteered several times to work in London to relieve girls there during the bombing raids. The London telegraph office, close to St. Paul's Cathedral, had been severely bombed and only one floor was left above ground. They worked there during the day, but at night they switched to machines that were below ground level, where they also slept and had their canteen.

DORIS:

Our town in Wales was invaded by about 10,000 American GIs. At the Post Office we handled telegrams by phone for the U.S. Army in nearby camps. Sometimes we worked on night shifts and, if it was quiet, we'd talk to the chaps in the (U.S. 811th) Signal Corps. One fellow, Rodrigus, said "How about meeting me for a

March 1945: Doris and Jack Amsbaugh

date?" I thought, there's safety in numbers, so I asked him if he had a "friend for my friend." We decided the four of us would meet. The blackout was in effect, so we met under the clock in the local railway station. There were two fellows standing under the clock--one was a short fellow and the other a tall blond. I took one look and decided I didn't care which one was Rodrigus, I was going to go with the tall blond. I did, and that was Jack!

My proper English mother insisted
that Jack needed pyjamas . . .

My family was surprised to see me dating a GI. When Jack came to the house, he brought canned food and my mother was especially pleased with a can of sausages as she used the surrounding fat for pie crusts. In return she gave Jack her one fresh egg-a-month ration for his breakfast. We dated about eighteen months before we married. When Jack proposed to me, he wasn't one to glamorize anything, and he painted such a gloomy picture of the States that I said, "By any chance are you hoping that I'll say NO?" I didn't! We were married 3 March 1945 at our Summerhill Baptist Church in Newport and went to the Palm Court Hotel in Torquay for our honeymoon. My proper English mother insisted that Jack needed pyjamas at the hotel, so she gave eight of her precious clothing coupons so Jack would have some to wear. Jack's buddies saw us off on our honeymoon at the railway station and gave us a bottle of champagne. The porter put us in a first class compartment and locked the door! Quite a feat on a crowded wartime train.

Jack was soon sent to the Continent with his outfit following Patton's army into Austria. Later, when the war ended, he sailed back to the States. By then our daughter, Diana, was born. In March 1946 I received my U.S. Army travel orders to go to Bournemouth for processing. My mother and sister came down there to see us off. It was really hard on them. When I think of what our parents must have gone through when we left. . . . It was different for us; we were young and anxious to get going. My sister was fourteen-years old, and she adored me--a big, older sister. And of course, they'd had baby Diana around for three months. We really didn't know whether we'd ever come back home again.

We sailed on the troop ship *Washington*. It was March, and it was a rough journey. We ran into a dreadful storm and before it was over I must have fainted. I remember someone kept repeating, "Let go of the baby!" I was in the ship's hospital for four days, and Diana stayed with me as I was nursing her. The day before we reached New York, they said that anyone still in the hospital would be taken by ambulance to a local hospital. Weak as I was, I got up. It was 27 March 1946 when we arrived.

I got on the Streamliner and travelled down south.

Jack was at the dock to meet us, and he saw Diana for the first time. We stayed at his sister's house on Staten Island. After a week Jack went back to Danville, Virginia (where he worked for the telephone company) to get the house he'd rented painted and cleaned up for us. Right after the war it was terribly hard to get housing, and the four-room house Jack found had no hot water or anything.

After I'd been at his sister's house for another week, I felt too homesick and lonely to stay longer; kind as his sister was, it was somebody else's house. I got on the Streamliner and traveled down south. It was hard to handle the luggage, and the money was strange. I went into the dining-car to have dinner, and there I was, knife and fork held in the English manner and eating that way. People stared. When I arrived in Danville, I was ready for anything.

It was hard to understand the accent of people in southern Virginia, and they didn't understand me either. I'd go to the store and ask for a pound of butter or cheese, and they'd look puzzled. Finally, I just pointed to the things I wanted. It wasn't self-service in those days. All my cookbook recipes were in English weight measures, not in cups, so, until I found a little weighing machine, I couldn't do much baking. Jack bragged about his mother's applesauce cake that was so moist it fell in the middle! It tasted good, but my mother would have had a fit if that happened to one of her cakes, and hers were moist enough.

I was still very homesick. After our daughter Susie was born, I took both girls with me to Wales to visit my family. That helped. Afterwards I never looked back. I became a citizen in 1953, and Jack's boss was my sponsor--although he told the judge "I doubt she'll take up arms for the United States against Britain!"

* * * * *

Doris and Jack fulfilled their expectations of a happy life together. The arrival of their grandchild, Michelle, was a special blessing to Jack before he became ill. He died of cancer a few years later.

26 May 1945: Outside St. Saviour's Church

John and Joan Walker with their wedding party.

Joan Atyeo lived in Weston-super-Mare, Somerset with her family and worked for Varley Pumps (a London Company that was evacuated to Weston) making parts for Spitfires. Posters there heralded visits to the factory by battle-scarred RAF pilots--**"Out Of The Blue To Talk To You!"** These visits were popular with the girls and did wonders for the workers' morale and production.

JOAN:
 Jack was in the U.S. Navy, and I met him at a dance. My friends and I would meet at the Grand Atlantic, a big elegant hotel on the sea-front in Weston-super-Mare, where we had a drink before going to a dance at the Winter Garden. Jack was there with a

| ... his mother called me "one of those bloody chirpers." |

group of U.S. naval officers, and they followed us to the Winter Garden. After eyeing each other a little, Jack came over and asked me to dance. That was it, as it turned out.

Jack was stationed at Dunkeswell, Devon. Actually, he never got around to proposing to me, but he did ask my parent's permission to marry me. Then Jack received orders to leave shortly, so we were married quickly, on 26 May 1945, after receiving special permission from the Bishop of Bath and Wells. I remember the white shoes I wore on my wedding day--I painted a black pair white! We spent a short honeymoon at the Old Bell Hotel, Exminster. Little did we know that we wouldn't meet again for over two years.

In February 1946 my travel orders arrived, and I was sent to the Salisbury Plain Camp at Tidworth. The worse part was lining up for a physical where you opened your robe and stood naked before an Army doctor. It was a shock to a young girl in those days, with no nurses around. It could have been done in a better way. I sailed on the *Queen Mary*. Conditions aboard were very crowded, and many were seasick. Five days later we reached New York City, and I was greeted by a telegram from Jack. He was a career officer in the U.S. Navy, and the message said he'd been sent to Okinawa! "Don't worry, the C.O. said it will be for only three months." But those months stretched into over a year.

If I had known then what I know now about the Navy, I would have gone back to England to wait for him. But I went to live with my in-laws in Detroit, Michigan, as Jack wanted. They were Canadian, of Scotch and Irish background, and I thought they'd be happy with an English daughter-in-law. His father was good to me, but his mother called me "one of those bloody chirpers." I got on well with my fifteen-year-old sister-in-law, but like most teenagers she didn't get along with her parents. I was in the middle, which wasn't good.

My in-laws didn't want me to work. They expected me to go to their Methodist church with them, and I did until I discovered an Episcopal church nearby and started attending services there. I felt much happier hearing the old familiar words spoken, but going to the Episcopal church caused some friction between me and my in-laws. I was befriended by an aunt of Angela Lansbury who had come

> There's a beautiful little church in the village where
> American sailors go every year for a special memorial service.

from London years before and she was wonderful to me. She and
other good friends helped soften things for me. Of course, things
got better once Jack returned from Okinawa. Then he went to
Northwestern University to finish his degree. Luckily, the Navy
sent us to England for three years' duty. You can tell how Jack
fitted in over there as my friends called him the "Squire."

We had three children. Jack's naval career meant that we
traveled extensively and lived in many foreign places. Jack couldn't
understand why I hesitated to become an American citizen. Once
we were delayed for ages after flying home from overseas duty,
waiting for an immigration inspector to see me, the only alien.
Our baby was fretful with an earache, and he was crying and
crying. Jack was really angry at me.

In the early 1960s, after much soul searching and tears, we
traded off: Jack would become an Episcopalian, and I would get
American citizenship. The judge at my ceremony told me that the
British were always the last ones to take out citizenship.

A few years ago Jack and I went back to Devon and visited
Dunkeswell where Jack had been stationed. It's now an RAF
parachute-jump school. There's a beautiful little church in the
village where American sailors go every year for a special
memorial service. They gave the church a new pipe organ. There's
also a plaque to Joseph Kennedy Jr. who was killed when his plane,
packed with explosives, accidently blew up before he reached his
target in northern France, the German's V-1 Buzz Bomb site
closest to England.

After Jack retired as a Naval officer, we were able to devote
more time to our family--and especially to our seven grandchildren. They call me "Nan," and as one of them put it, "she sounds
like that because she's from England."

* * * * *

Joan and Jack celebrated their Golden Wedding anniversary by going
on a sentimental cruise to England aboard the *Queen Elizabeth* II. There
they paid a special visit to St. Saviour's Church, where they were married
in 1945, to receive a Thanksgiving Blessing by the Vicar.

AMERICAN RED CROSS CLUBS

Sent to England early in the war, anthropologist Margaret Mead had wondered what the GIs would do in their free time, when all of Britain lacked the wholesome "corner drug stores with soda fountains" so popular back home. One of the answers lay in the opening of 265 American Red Cross clubs throughout the United Kingdom with the cooperation of the British government. Not publicized was the fact that British Reverse Lend-Lease paid for most of the premises and equipment used by the American Red Cross. From mid-1942 until the war ended in 1945, ARC personnel working in the ETO (European Theater of Operations) successfully operated clubs offering a myriad of free home-style "rest and recreation" services to GIs. And for just a few pennies, soft drinks, donuts, light meals, and beds were theirs. The ARC sought out the help of thousands of carefully selected British employees (who had to buy ARC uniforms or smocks), as well as volunteers, to serve in many different ways. For young girls, the most exciting volunteer job was "dance hostess" in one of those service clubs.

After VE-Day, in June 1945, Mrs. Sloan Colt, Deputy Commissioner of the American Red Cross in Great Britain, sent a hearty "thank you" letter from her office on Grosvenor Square to all of those volunteers. She appreciated the long hours they had "spent working at information desks, in First Aid rooms, in canteens, snackbars, sewing on buttons and stripes, driving ARC cars, and dancing innumerable miles" with American servicemen. The latter is where I came in, and I was pleased to receive one of her letters.

London had eleven ARC Service Clubs for enlisted men, two for servicewomen and four Officers' Clubs scattered around the city. They all had facilities that offered information, food, recreation, free theatre tickets, dancing, and a place to sleep. Open twenty-four hours a day, the largest club was Rainbow Corner at ever-busy Piccadilly Circus. **"If you get lost in London come here,"** GIs were advised on a map of London distributed by the ARC. One of the smallest clubs was located in a quiet area on Hans Crescent Road in Knightsbridge.

Vera Cracknell, age seventeen, from Alperton, Middlesex

VERA:
I had been invited as a guest to go to a tea-dance at the Hans Crescent American Red Cross Club near Harrods in Knightsbridge. A letter from Mid Eberly, ARC, arrived soon afterward asking me to volunteer there as a Junior Hostess. My mother had a fit until I explained that it was quite proper--plus the unrationed food available there meant a lot. I had to have photos taken and was even checked by Scotland Yard. Kathleen (Kick) Kennedy was a Red Cross girl at Hans Crescent, and I remember the excitement at the club (6 May 1944) when she married Billy Hartington, the Duke of Devonshire's son. Her brother, Joseph Kennedy Jr., was at the

> ### "Just take what they say to you with a pinch of salt!"

wedding. Tragically, after D-Day, Kick's new husband, Billy, and Joe Kennedy Jr. were both killed in action.

I met Charles Long at one of the dances at Hans Crescent. He was from Kingston, Pennsylvania, stationed in London, with U.S. Army Signal Intelligence. It was a few weeks before D-Day 1944, and I was wearing a new red dress that I had splurged precious clothing coupons on. My older sister thought it was too festive for those war years, but later on, Charles remembered that it was "nifty--the dress with the brass rivets!" We met, danced together and it was love.

My mother had warned me not to get serious with any of the Yanks. "Just take what they say to you with a pinch of salt!" Anyhow, Charles came home for tea and to meet my mother. She gave him baked-beans on toast with a cup of tea, which he thought was strange. We were so strictly rationed, there wasn't much choice. He brought me some Rubinstein's "Heaven Sent" perfume.

Soon after D-Day we were being attacked by the pilotless V-1s, and later by the even more scary V-II rockets that zipped from the sky without any warning. Charles and I dated until he was sent to Paris in September 1944, and by then we were seriously considering marriage.

We wrote to each other every day, and I also corresponded with his family in the States. His father had died while he was stationed in England, and Charles considered it his responsibility to help support his mother. It wasn't going to be easy, but he had a government job to return to, and we'd live in Washington, D.C.

When the war ended, Charles, who was in Germany, obtained permission for us to get married in England before he would be sent back to the States. In late October he suddenly appeared at our house, a year since we'd seen one another. He brought me a lovely diamond engagement ring, sent by his family in the States-- and a box of cigars for our wedding! He said it was easier to carry cigars than champagne, both available at his PX. Two days later, 27 October 1945, we were married at St. James' Church, Alperton. My sister Hilda, whose husband was in the RAF, added more excitement for our family when her first baby arrived at about the same time, so the cigars came in handy for them. Charles and I

. . . "Charles, I see your package has arrived!"

spent our honeymoon in Bournemouth. The ARC found us a place
to stay, a lovely old Tudor house called Maxims Hotel. *Heavenly!*
    In January 1946 Charles sailed home to the States and civilian
life. My travel orders arrived in March, and I was sent first to
Tidworth. It was very emotional leaving my mother, family, and
friends, but I was torn with excitement and desire to get going
once the time had arrived. At Tidworth, German prisoners-of-war
dished out American style food, including corn that we'd never
eaten before. We had PX privileges and bought scarce items such
as sweets and cigarettes to send to our families, but that was not
allowed, so three of us went "out of bounds" and walked to a
village, mailed our treasures and even phoned home. We sailed
from Southampton on the giant liner *Queen Mary.* I shared a tiny
cabin with three women and their babies. The ship was filled with
GI brides, children and a few first-class passengers.
    We docked in New York on 4 April 1946, right before Easter.
Charles met me on the pier, and, after spending a couple of days
at the Dixie Hotel--and trying to sample all the fresh juice and
bananas I could--we took a Martz bus to Wilkes Barre, Pennsylvania to meet his family. They made me very welcome, but the
louder his family chatted about local things and "Easter bonnets,"
the quieter I became. I was so shy, I sat studiously knitting a scarf.
Someone said, "Charles, I see your package has arrived!" And I was
teased about "beating the British" during the Revolutionary War.
No one talked about what had just happened in Europe: beating
the Nazis, something I'd grown up with for seven years. I was dis-
mayed to have it completely ignored, and I felt lonely and homesick.
    We left by bus for Washington, D.C., where Charles worked
part-time for the government while attending George Washington
University. The city was still overcrowded from the war, and
apartments were scarce. We were lucky to find a room for rent in
a private house, but we had to share the bathroom and eat all our
meals out. I soon put on weight when I found that I could get
cream, instead of milk, with my breakfast cereal at the corner
drugstore. Initially, the city, with its classical white buildings and
beautiful surroundings, seemed too flawless and "sterile" to me. I
suppose in contrast to the grubby and bombed-out buildings I was
used to seeing in London. The only messy spot I remember was

where wads of chewing gum had bonded onto the sidewalk in front of the Capital Theater (movie house) on F Street.

I found a secretarial job after several setbacks and being surprised at some prejudice against "brides from Britain." I worked for the American Council on Education and was earning $50 a week when I left, nearly two years later, to have my first baby. I loved staying at home while raising our four children.

Before that, in the autumn of 1946, I was excited when my sister Hilda, Bill and baby emigrated to Canada. We planned a Christmas reunion with them in Toronto and traveled on a crowded overnight train from Washington, D.C. to Buffalo, N.Y. There we got a train to Toronto. Comfortably seated, a Canadian Immigration officer came around and asked where we were born. I produced my British passport (not stamped, having entered the U.S. under the *War Brides Act*) and was told, "You're welcome to enter Canada but you'll need a border-crossing card to re-enter the States." What a shock! He stopped the train for us to get off before it crossed the border at Black Rock junction. It was a snowy desolate spot, bitterly cold and not even a station there. Soon, however, another train stopped to pick us up on its way back to Niagara Falls, N.Y. We phoned Hilda, then made our way to Pennsylvania, where Charles' mother lived. Christmas Eve we knocked on her door. Surprise! It was hard to explain why we had been "thrown off" the train. The following May, comfortable in a Pullman sleeper and with a border crossing card tucked safely in my bag, we made it to Toronto for our delayed reunion.

In 1947, my mother and aunt had the trip of their lives when they flew across the Atlantic to visit us, and then had a fantastic train trip across America for a reunion in California with their sister Pat, whom they hadn't seen in thirty years.

Our family now includes five lovely grandchildren. They know what Boxing Day, Figgy Pudding (with silver charms) and Christmas Crackers are. Charles' mother was puzzled the first holiday season she spent with us, when I made a fuss about finding Christmas crackers. She thought they were just something to eat. It became our family tradition to "pop" festive crackers containing prizes and funny paper hats to wear for Christmas dinner.

I felt proud in 1988 when our family came to George Mason University to see me, "Graduating Granny," get a degree in history, with honors. Best of all, though, is the undying love that Charles and I still have for each other.

USO: UNITED SERVICE ORGANIZATIONS

The USO, with headquarters in New York City, was organized in 1941 and consisted of six national social service agencies: the Young Men's Christian Associations; the National Catholic Community Service; the Salvation Army; the Young Women's Christian Associations; the National Jewish Welfare Board and the National Travelers Aid Association.

In London, Eileen Wright worked for USO Camp Shows, as the USO was known in Britain during the Second World War. It provided entertainment for the troops. She felt that there was "fierce rivalry between the USO and the American Red Cross (ARC)" which earlier had organized overseas recreation and services for "the boys" serving with the U.S. Armed Forces.

The ARC was supposed to let the USO provide entertainment through Camp Shows, and the USO, in turn, was to stay out of providing coffee, doughnuts and recreational activities. USO Camp Shows observed the rules, but the ARC sometimes also put on shows of its own, much to the displeasure of USO performers who didn't like to face an almost empty theatre because the ARC had given a show the night before.

Organizing USO concerts involved many people. Transportation to the bases was arranged by U.S. Army Special Service. Base locations and the numbers of troops to be entertained were restricted information. Eileen's office arranged "hotel accommodations, collected and forwarded pay, acted as nursemaids and soothed egos." They were responsible for hiring artistes in London, "often minor stage personalities," to appear with popular British stars like Bebe Daniels and Ben Lyons. Celebrity troupes, that included stars such as Bob Hope and Sam Levene, were organized in America. In her spare time Eileen was busy studying voice and music, preparing to take exams for certification.

EILEEN:

Van Karten and I met early in 1945 when I walked into his office in Brook Street, London, with a package of drawings of wounded American servicemen which had to pass the censor before being mailed to servicemen's families in the U.S.A. Van was an officer with Military Intelligence, and his duties included debriefing Allied pilots who had "ditched" in the North Sea, rescued by the Swedes and returned to the U.K.

I was only nineteen years old when I met Van, and he was a thirty-five-year-old bachelor. My family was not pleased. Van's family in the States was not pleased either. In spite of this, our relationship became more important to us as time passed (actually, we were both deeply in love), and we have never had cause to regret it. A year after we met, and with the war over, my parents gave their permission for me to marry Van. He was in Germany by then, but in spite of that he managed to arrive at the church on time. We were married 18 March 1946 at St. Luke's Church, London.

**Eileen Wright from Clapham Common, London
and Van Karten, U.S. Army**

> We were on the top floor . . . two rooms plus a white and gold
> bathroom with paintings of nymphs being pursued by centaurs.

Seven months later, in October, I said "good-bye" to my family
and boarded the boat train to Paris on the first leg of my journey
to join Van in Kulmbach, Germany. From Paris I was put on an
overnight train to Frankfurt. As a Londoner I knew what bombing
could do, but nothing prepared me for the devastation I found
here. Everything was bombed, grey and smelled of cabbage. People
emerged and disappeared into holes in the rubble where they had
sturdy underground shelters.

From Frankfurt, transportation became difficult because more
and more Allied dependents were arriving in Germany. It had
become clear that German de-Nazification and Allied help in
rebuilding and stabilizing the country would take many years.
Besides, there was the growing Russian threat.

The U.S. military had a system to handle families coming from
the States, and they were either met at Bremerhaven or put on
trains in groups to their final destination. I, however, was a lone
traveler presenting myself at an unscheduled time to the Rail
Transportation Officer with orders for Kulmbach. I was routed to
devastated Nuremberg where the station was teeming with the
homeless. A visit to the restroom resulted in two people being
ordered out of their shelter in the stall by an officious woman
with a broom. From Nuremberg I was sent to Bamberg and from
there to Bayreuth. I was usually alone in a compartment reserved
for members of the Allied Forces. In the other compartments,
travelers were squeezed in like sardines with the over-flow clinging
to the outside of the train. At Bayreuth I was informed that the
train to Kulmbach would not leave until the next day. I asked
(begged) the RTO to try to reach Van by telephone which he did.
Van arrived an hour later. He was frantic with worry about me,
and I was very tired of the exciting world of postwar train travel.

In Kulmbach, we were quartered in the mansion of a local
magnate who owned a large fabric mill. We were on the top floor
in the old servants' quarters--very plush--two rooms plus a white
and gold bathroom with oil paintings of nymphs being pursued
by centaurs.

> . . . Ilse Koch, who was accused, among other crimes,
> of having made lamp shades from human skin.

Earlier arrivals had staked out the two master bedroom suites and other guest rooms. Butler, cook, cleaning and kitchen maids were provided. Meals were served in the dining room. There was a library, sitting room, reception room with fireplace and grand piano, ballroom, study, grand foyer, various nooks and a solarium with a view of the extensive grounds. We also had a view of a camp which housed displaced persons and was formerly occupied by slave labor from all over Europe. The mansion was also used as an Officers' Club, and every Saturday night people came to dinner and stayed to play cards. The Colonel's wife, a glamorous ex-model and a "she who must be obeyed" type, liked to wear her strapless gowns at formal dinner parties. We disliked these command performances.

In May 1947, Van was assigned to Pullach, near Munich. There we lived in another mansion where Martin Bormann, Hitler's deputy, had formerly lived. Again, we were assigned to the servants' quarters and had meals served in the dining room. By this time, I longed to be in a place of our own, and finally we were given quarters in an apartment in the compound.

While in Pullach, I visited the site of the Dachau concentration camp which had been liberated by the American 3rd Army on 29 April 1945, freeing about 30,000 survivors. The cremation ovens were left intact as a memorial, but the rest of the camp was razed and barracks erected to house displaced persons. Just two weeks prior to the liberation of Dachau, U.S. troops had freed the concentration camp at Buchenwald, near Jena.

In the summer of 1947 when I visited Dachau, the legal branch of the U.S. Military Government was conducting a trial of Nazi SS troopers captured at Buchenwald, including the Commandant's wife, Ilse Koch, who was accused among other crimes of having made lamp shades from human skin. The conduct of the trial was a painstaking process involving the translation of testimony from and into English, German, French, Polish and Russian, depending upon the native tongue of the witness. The accused sat in a row, mostly expressionless and looking like people you pass in a crowd. Ilse Koch managed to

> ... "Pancake Tuesdays" have always been
> a big hit in our family.

become pregnant while in solitary confinement, causing a lot of ribald speculation about the possible identity of the father.

While on leave in the States in 1949, I became a U.S. citizen under the provision of a law which dispensed with the U.S. residence requirement for foreign spouses of military personnel. Our four children, two girls and twin boys, were all born in Germany. We remained there until 1967. After spending twenty-one years in post-war Germany, we sailed from Cherbourg to America on one of the last transatlantic crossings of the *United States*. Van continued to work for the Army Security Agency until he retired in 1980.

I didn't have the problem adjustment to life in the U.S. that many other GI brides experienced because I was somewhat prepared for it by our stay in Germany. I had learned a lot from American military wives, from newspapers and so on.

I have always been fortunate to find other "Brits" no matter where we have gone, and their friendship has meant a lot to me. As far as traditions go, "Pancake Tuesdays" have always been a big hit in our family.

My mother died in 1962, and it was years before we went back to England again. Then I felt as though I had come from another planet. What happened to Lyon's Corner Houses? Even fish and chip shops were not the same.

DIVORCE

Like peacetime marriages, some wartime marriages encountered difficulties. Most of the overseas GI marriages that seemed to be doomed to failure ended in divorce within the first few years. According to 1946 American Red Cross records, those failed marriages numbered about 6,000, English-Speaking Union statistics for the same period showed 2,600 divorces, and other figures fall somewhere in between. There are no cut-and-dried numbers, but the figure is less than eight per cent of 60,000 marriages.

Some war brides were still living overseas and expecting to sail to America when they were notified that their GI husbands had divorced them in a U.S. Court. Or the girls themselves, in some cases, had decided that they could not leave their familiar environment and homeland after all, and a divorce followed.

For a couple who had been reunited in the States but soon divorced, it was usually the GI husband, rarely the war bride, who sued to break up the marriage. Most of the girls came from working and middle-class backgrounds, and very few of them had financial means of their own. Jobs were scarce for married women in those days when GI veterans were returning to the work force. Besides, it was thought that a wife's place was in the home! The war bride trapped in an unhappy marriage without money of her own was at a further disadvantage. She had no family nearby for support and advice. It took guts and a measure of independence for such a newcomer to America, someone like Jean Holder Carter, to even contemplate a divorce. Jean had become so disillusioned with her marriage that she separated from her husband, worked hard and saved enough money to go to Reno, Nevada (the "U.S. Divorce Capital" at the time) where she established a six-weeks residency in order to get her divorce.

Jean Holder hailed from Battersea, London and as a school girl in 1939, when the war started, she was evacuated to the country. She later returned home and worked as a shorthand typist for Elder Reed & Co. in Battersea. Jean volunteered to serve as a firewatcher during the Blitz, then as an air-raid warden until she qualified to be a Red Cross nurse. She remembers vividly what happened next.

JEAN:

In 1943 I met Bill Carter who was a U.S. Army Air Corps pilot stationed in England. We met while I was on holiday in Cornwall, and we were married in March 1944, several months later. Bill was sent back to the States a week after our wedding, and I made plans to join him there. It took nearly a year, however, before I could leave wartime England.

Early in 1945, with emigration papers in order, including a valid passport and visa (required before the *War Brides Act,* 28 December 1945 went into effect) I managed to get space on the *Mauretania* sailing in a convoy from Liverpool to New York. The war was still being fought, and the ship carried hundreds of wounded servicemen and about 130 other GI brides, some with children. In addition to my fare of 150 pounds sterling for the voyage, I had to pre-purchase a train voucher for use in the States once I had arrived. We landed in February 1945. I had not heard from Bill in recent months, so reached America not knowing exactly where he was.

The American Red Cross in New York City helped several of us to find a hotel room the first night and gave each of us three dollars. I used my train voucher to travel to Trenton, New Jersey, where the parents of Bill's best friend lived. They took me in and I stayed with them for several weeks while trying to locate Bill in the Army Air Corps.

I had a great-aunt living in Atlantic City, so next I went there, got an office job at $25 a week and lived in a rooming house for $10 a week.

Eventually, I located Bill and found he was living with another woman. Still, Bill and I decided to make a fresh start together in what was a very tenuous relationship. Bill was still in the service, and together we crisscrossed the country many times those first years. Finally, in 1951, I called it quits, went to Reno, Nevada and divorced Bill. After that I concentrated on my career in Washington, D.C. and succeeded in making an excellent life for myself in America.

WAR BRIDES ACROSS AMERICA

The foreign born war brides, many of whom arrived in America with skilled work experience and special talents, soon contributed to the economy of the country. They occupied a variety of jobs, and, in the fashion of the times stayed at home when raising their families. Together with their husbands, they required new homes and schools for their children who were part of the postwar "Baby Boom."

On 20 January 1946, in discussing the number of war brides from Great Britain, the *New York Times* column "Topic of Times" editorialized that "this new aggregate American population of husbands, wives and children is not far from twice the population of California when it entered the Union in 1850." One hundred years after the Golden State was born, those thousands of war brides mentioned in the *Times* column did much more than add figures to the population. They fostered international relations through correspondence with family and friends, travel, trade and the exchange of social customs.

When the inevitable feelings of homesickness threatened, so common among all immigrants, it helped many of these these young women to have a cup of tea and a "natter" (chat) with a fellow Britisher. Neighborhoods, schools, churches, businesses and organizations such as the Transatlantic Brides and Parents Association (TBPA) aided the girls in finding one another.

"The British are coming!" shouted Paul Revere over two centuries ago when some of the 30,000 Hessian mercenaries, hired by Royal forces, appeared to fight during the Revolutionary War. It was following World War II, however, that a fleet of ships finally brought thousands who really were British to American shores. Where are they now? Seven of those war brides--Ada, Dorothy, Doreen, Eileen, Iris, Nancy and Doris--each born in a different English county, live in places scattered around the U.S.A. They know each other through the TBPA network, and through their diverse stories we also know something about them. Those who served in His Majesty's Forces during World War II share their memories later.

"Where Are They Now?"

This is Ada Dimmock's story. She lived in Derby, Derbyshire, and her
September 1942 marriage to a GI, Jim Donellan, U.S. Army, was one of
the earliest to occur in England. After the war, Ada went to Baton Rouge,
Louisiana, to join her husband, and she still lives there.

ADA:
   In 1942 I met Jim at a church club. It was cold, and they were
serving hot tea. He asked me for a date, and I agreed, but, knowing
how strict my mother and dad were, I tried to lose him on the way
home but couldn't. We kept meeting and soon fell in love.
   It didn't take Jim long to get permission for us to get married
because he was a friend of the Captain. We were married in
September 1942 at St. Peters, our small local church. We only had
a couple of days together, no honeymoon, and then he was gone.
He was in the U.S. Army's 171st Railroad outfit and was sent to
North Africa.
   Our daughter, Mary, was born the following year, but it wasn't
until March 1946, nearly four years after Jim and I first met and
married that Mary and I were able to go to America. We were sent
to Tidworth first. The doctors checked us for lice and disease. I
think the American officer who fingerprinted us and put tags on
us, was rude.
   I was shipped out on the *Washington*, and during the voyage I
had my twenty-first birthday. We arrived 30 March in New York
City. Jim met us, and then we went by train to Baltimore where
Jim's aunt lived. My Irish Catholic father-in-law was also there,
and he insisted that we should marry again. "To make it legal!" he
said. Then we went to Jim's home in Baton Rouge. The first thing I
had to get used to in Louisiana was the heat, then the food and
then my in-laws. My mother-in-law would call me, "a pale face
English bitch," so it was rough for years, but I stuck it out.
   I've been here since 1946, and my sisters-in-law never had
anything to do with me. I felt like an outcast, I think lots of
English girls, the GI brides, were mistreated. If I had to do it all
over, I would say "No way."
   It's been a hard life. My family in England missed me, and Jim's
family wished I had never come. Jim was a hard worker, but he was

| The good has overtaken the bad. |

in the middle, his mother one side and me the other. They didn't like Jim marrying an English girl instead of an American. Once I invited two English engineers from Exxon Co., who were visiting the United States to come for a cup of tea. When they found out how badly I was treated, they told me to go back to England; British people don't mistreat others like that.

My dearest Jim is dead now; so are his parents. We had five children and now I've got twenty-seven grandkids and seven great-grandkids. It took me years, but I can finally say I am happy. Yes, I do tell my children and grandchildren about England. They love to hear my stories about me growing up there. I told them I was in a school play, *Peter Pan*, and you know who I was--the Dog. I had the teacher's fur coat on. They laugh and say "Ma! Ma! Please tell me another story." I also wrote a poem about my childhood home in Derby, and it's published in the *World Book of Poems*. Belonging to TBPA, a British Heritage Society, is important to me.

I became an American citizen in 1952, the year my mother died, so I have dual citizenship. I fly the British flag and now go back to visit once a year. The good has overtaken the bad. With my wonderful family, life is worthwhile.

February 1943: Dorothy and Edwin
Just Engaged!

Lancashire lass, Dorothy Sephton from Litherland, married Edwin Ferguson, U.S. Army, on 10 July 1943. After the war, Dorothy left the lively, crowded Liverpool area to live with her southern "Yank" husband on a farm in the wide open spaces near his home town, Brownwood, Texas.

DOROTHY:

We met in November, 1942 when I was nineteen years old. I was working as an "usherette" at a cinema theatre called the Winter Gardens in Waterloo. A good-looking Yank named Edwin Ferguson used to come to the theatre about twice a week. He was stationed at the Esplanade there in Waterloo. At first, he said he did not want to get involved, but when I got off work at 10:30 p.m. he was always outside waiting for me. Love bloomed! I worked at the cinema until we got married the following year.

Edwin and I became engaged in February, 1943, and we were married that same year on 10 July at St. Andrew's Church in Litherland, Liverpool. We spent our honeymoon in historic Stratford-on-Avon for one week.

Our daughter was born 31 October 1944, and, when she was seventeen months old, I received our travel orders to go to America. It was March 1946 when we left home for Tidworth, and after the formalities there we sailed on the *Holbrook*. On 8 April 1946 we arrived in New York City. The Red Cross was helpful and put us on a train to Texas. It was a long, tiring journey--we arrived in Brownwood five days later. My husband was there waiting for us. Edwin was in the process of buying a house when we arrived. We lived with his parents on their farm for six months and then moved into our own house. All these years later, we're still living there.

My in-laws were very good to me, and we didn't have any problems. The hardest thing that I had to get used to was the hot summers in Texas. Even today I still don't care for the heat. Edwin was a self-employed carpenter. We've been happily married for over fifty years now and take joy in our four children, nine grandchildren and two great-grandchildren. Our children gave us an exciting Golden wedding anniversary reception complete with surprises from England when my brother and his wife walked in, also my cousin (who had served as maid of honour in our wedding) and her husband. You can imagine the tears and the happy memories we shared with them.

Recently I retired after working for thirty-two years in the high school cafeteria. I am really going to miss the kids there. I have returned to England many times since I left home in 1946, and, just like all those years ago, it's always hard to let it go.

"You Yanks are taking our girls!"

Doreen Timmins lived with her family in Tenterden, Kent. She worked and was also a fire watcher during air raids. Doreen remembers how the skies were often full of war planes and how German planes would jettison unused bombs on their area after raiding London. During the Battle of Britain, many "dog fights" took place overhead. Sadly, her youngest brother, who was one of Churchill's "Few" in the Royal Air Force, was killed at that time.

Later, American Flying Fortresses used to group overhead, using Tenterden Church as a landmark, going back and forth to bomb Germany. During that period, Doreen met Paul Kriegler who came from Buffalo, New York and was serving with the U.S. Army 8th Air Force in England.

DOREEN:

I met Paul in October 1943 soon after his Flying Fortress was forced to make an emergency landing at High Halden when returning from a bombing run over Germany. The air crews repaired their own planes, if possible, and, while they waited for a replacement part, they were in the care of the local British military. My friend, Captain James Dickinson, introduced me to Paul at a Town Hall dance. We had several dates before the crew flew back to their base in Honington, Suffolk.

Paul came to see me again--with the help of Capt. Dickinson since we were in a restricted area. When Paul and I were leaving a dance, a British Army lad said, "You Yanks are taking our girls!"

We had fallen in love and decided to get married. Paul filled out papers to prove that he could pay my fare to the States and to support me. We had a lovely white wedding at St. Mildred's Church, Tenterden. After the wedding reception, we had a week's honeymoon at The Swan, Tunbridge Wells and at the Russell Square Hotel, London. When checking into the hotels, Paul was asked to show proof that we were married and not "shacking up!"

Shortly after D-Day, Paul was sent to France. In Kent, we were in the staging area for D-Day troops assembling to go to southern ports, and we heard the coastal guns when the Normandy invasion started. Germany soon retaliated by aiming V-I buzz bombs at Britain. We learned to listen for the engine to stop and then the awful explosion when it fell.

29 March 1944: Paul and Doreen on their wedding day

When the war ended, Paul returned to the States while I waited in England for passage to join him. After two years I was on my way, going first to Tidworth, a phase I tolerated. We sailed from Southampton on the *Bridgeport*, a First World War hospital ship used by the Germans. There were ten girls in our cabin. Volunteers worked in the nurseries and on the ship's newspaper. We were

| A sign indicated we were "GI wives and families." |

subject to propaganda giving the impression that we were to be granted a great favor by being allowed into the U.S.A.

All I wanted was to be with my husband. On 6 April 1946, after sixteen rough days at sea, we landed in New York.

Due to Red Cross misinformation, Paul went to New York City before our ship arrived and then returned to Buffalo to await notice of the correct date. He never received it, so I was put ashore after all the others had left, then taken to Grand Central Station for a train to Niagara Falls. It was disappointing not to find Paul waiting. Sad also to be put into a cordoned off area in the station with other "unmet" wives and children. A sign indicated we were "GI wives and families." Passers-by stared at this sign and us. No doubt we looked a sorry bunch. After a long train ride Paul and I finally had our reunion.

I found Paul's family very different, but they made me welcome. I had difficulty getting used to so much food after years of strict rationing in England. At first we had to live with my in-laws, and the lack of privacy was difficult for me. I wanted to talk to my family, but overseas phone calls were a luxury back then.

In 1947 we moved to our own place in Wilson, New York, and two years later our daughter, Lyn, was born. Karan arrived in 1954. I've kept up some British traditions, talking to the children and making special foods at Christmas. Keeping in touch with others from Britain is easier through our TBPA club. We keep the "flag flying" on many special occasions. I was pleased to be given a Life Membership for my work in TBPA.

We retired and lived in England for six exciting years, but we are now back in Virginia, living not far from Karan and family. We enjoy seeing our three grandchildren growing up. Lyn married a New Zealander and lives in Auckland, so we seldom see her, but we're always in touch. She's a well-known illustrator for children's books there and has been honored by receiving prestigious awards in New Zealand and Britain.

In 1995, as a World War II GI bride from Kent, I was interviewed by the BBC about my romance and what life was like during the war, for a special radio program, "Wartime Kent."

Finally, after all these years, I became an American citizen--just in time for our fiftieth wedding anniversary celebration.

1945: Eileen and Bill Racy
All Saints Church, Newmarket, Suffolk

On 29 April 1945, Eileen Fordham from Newmarket, Suffolk married Oscar (Bill) Racy, U.S. Army 8th Air Force, from Cherryvale, Kansas.

Eileen left Newmarket, famous since early in the 17th century for horse racing, merry King Charles II and the sporting set, and moved to her new home in Kansas where the State Song "Home on the Range" promised love and contentment. It worked!

EILEEN:

In late summer 1944 I met my Yank, Bill, at a ballroom in Newmarket. I was sixteen years old and worked as a clerk in a Solicitor's office. He was twenty-two and in the 8th Air Force, 94th Bomb Group, stationed at Rougham, near Bury St. Edmunds, where he worked on the "line" doing sheet metal repairs on B-17 bombers.

By Christmas we were talking marriage but faced considerable opposition from my parents who thought I was much too young to get married and go so far from home. Later, I realized how right they were, but at the time I couldn't be convinced. On my seventeenth birthday they finally agreed, and after all the U.S. Army red tape we were married on 29 April 1945 at All Saints Church, Newmarket.

We spent our honeymoon at the Regent Palace Hotel, London, near Piccadilly Circus, and it was the most public honeymoon in history! Every day guys from the base dropped in on us, and the last five days we were joined by my sister, Sybil, and her husband John, on embarkation leave from the RAF. One day, toward the end of our stay, we all became ill from food poisoning and were lying across the bed trying to recuperate, when we heard people in the street below shouting that the war with Germany was over. Victory in Europe!

It didn't take us long to pull ourselves together and go down to join the throngs who were gathering to celebrate. And what a celebration--a blur of hugging, dancing and singing. In the cold light of dawn we decided that the crowds would only get worse, so we returned to Newmarket to finish the celebration with our family.

Bill stayed in England until September 1945 when he returned home and was discharged. I awaited a ship to the States. It seemed like a long winter, even with frequent letters until early in February 1946 I was sent to Tidworth camp--and again contracted food poisoning. Fortunately, our ship was delayed for a few days, and by then I was well enough to make it on board. Our voyage on the *Vulcania* wasn't too comfortable. We carried life jackets at all times as mines still posed a danger, and we saw quite a few icebergs. Everything was far from luxurious, but we were soon going to see our husbands, and after months of waiting, nothing else mattered.

> **I asked my mother-in-law where I could wash out some undies . . . "in the lavatory!"**

Bill met me in New York, and it was a shock seeing him in civilian clothes! The U.S. Army would have transported me all the way to Kansas, but I had an uncle in New Jersey who was anxious to see me, and, since they wouldn't let him take me from the ship, he called Bill to come to New York. Afterward, we had quite a hairy trip driving to Kansas, especially going through a blizzard in Pennsylvania. I kept seeing bunches of bananas hanging from roadside stands, but we were always going too fast to stop. When we finally reached Cherryvale and his folks' home, there wasn't a banana in the house. After going seven years without bananas, waiting another day didn't hurt.

One of the hardest adjustments I had to make was calling my husband Oscar instead of Bill. He hated his first name and used Bill while in the service. Back home though, Bill was his father's name, and everyone called my husband Oscar. I was also confused over language differences. Soon after I arrived I asked my mother-in-law where I could wash some undies. She told me "in the lavatory." I thought she meant the toilet! We bought a little house in Cherryvale and have lived there ever since, building on and remodeling as our three children came along.

Homesickness was terribly hard on me, especially in the early years. It was eight years before I could make my first trip home and then, fortunately, I made several more trips while my parents were still alive. Bill worked for the Santa Fe Railroad after the war, and then for the Burlington Northern until his retirement. Our own family has grown in size and now includes four grandchildren. Wonderful!

Iris Barber met and dazzled Bob Batten from Houston, Texas

Iris Barber, from Swindon, calls herself a "Moonraker," a legendary Wiltshire name that was coined when some local smugglers were retrieving casks of contraband whisky--using long poles with hooks--from a moonlit pond. Suddenly, excise men surprised them. When asked what they were doing, one quick-witted smuggler pointed to the reflection of the moon on the pond and said in typical yokel fashion, "We be fishin' for that there cheese." The tax agents, thinking they were dealing with halfwits, burst out laughing and rode away. So the "Moonrakers" had the last laugh, and the tale lives on.

During World War II Iris was a stenographer for the Great Western Railway. A professionally trained singer, Iris sang with a ladies choir that competed successfully at Eistedfodds in Wales. Later, they loved singing at U.S. Army hospitals, where the cooks supplied them with scarce canned foods. Iris remembers her singing teacher, "dear Mrs. Parsons," and her favorite admonishment: "The tip of the tongue, the teeth and the lips."

IRIS:
I was twenty years old when James Robbie (Bob) Batten, U.S. Army 9th Air Force, age twenty-four, entered my life. It was at a roller skating rink. He was stationed at Membury some fourteen miles away, and on his first evening in Swindon, while wandering around in the blackout, he came to the skating rink. He wasn't going to skate until he saw my best friend Nora and me skating as a duo around and around. He followed us for awhile and then skated up to us, caught hold of my arm but looked at Nora and said to her, "You've had her long enough--let me have her for awhile." Famous last words! Years later and we're still together.

We really had a rocky-road-to-romance as he was always being sent off somewhere, and, not having a telephone, he'd send me an "express" letter which always arrived after he'd returned. I was fascinated! Here was someone who didn't care a scrap for my singing, wasn't musical, didn't turn up for dates most of the time and he didn't woo me with candy bars and nylon hose. Once, he did give me a couple of oranges that he didn't want. On top of that he was very handsome. How could I resist? And opposites do attract.

When Bob was sent to France shortly after D-Day in 1944, we wrote every day. I still have one smaltzy twenty-five pager he wrote me in a weak moment. We got engaged by mail and arranged to get married 22 June 1945. On the first day of June the phone rang where I was working. It was Bob calling from London. "Can you get married in 48 hours because that's all I've got. I'm going on to the Pacific!" I hadn't seen him for eleven months.

I met his train and we rushed off to the registry office and arranged to get married at 9:30 the next morning, 2 June 1945. No time for a church wedding or to wear my white wedding dress. Not having a phone, I stopped off at a co-worker's house to tell

If you'd like to call your husband, I'll hold the train!

her, and I was thrilled when in addition to my parents the whole office staff turned up for the wedding. In fact, the office manager was best man, and my boss was matron of honor. On the way to the registry office, Bob popped into a greengrocer's shop to get me a bouquet, a dozen (old) red carnations wrapped up, slimy stems and all, in newspaper--drip, drip all through the ceremony. There were twelve of us, so everyone got a carnation, and we rushed off to London for a very short honeymoon. The next day Bob flew back to Germany, and I didn't see him again until I reached Texas the following year.

I left Swindon in February 1946 for Tidworth with Maureen McQueen whom I knew slightly and is now a good friend. Our voyage on the *Argentina* took eight days. Both the *Washington* and the *Queen Mary* left after we did, and both beat us in. We arrived 2 March 1946 in New York. The Red Cross had assured us that they would notify our husbands of our arrival and not to spend money on telegrams. It was a three-day train journey to Houston, via St. Louis, where the other GI brides got off, so I was alone. However, the other passengers were wonderful to me. Except one lady who said "Oh, you're one of those English girls who married our boys; my daughter would hate you!" One couple across from me glared at her, and they took me under their wing. So did two American girls who gave me the perfect manicure to arrive with.

Meanwhile, the nice train conductor told me "We'll be pulling into Little Rock, Arkansas at 11 p.m. If you'd like to call your husband, I'll hold the train!" At Little Rock I rushed to a phone booth, followed by the friendly couple with coins in their hands. I got Bob immediately. He had no idea I had even left England. When we arrived in Houston, there he was, looking handsome in his civilian clothes, carnation corsage in hand and flanked by his two sisters and their husbands. Incidentally, the Red Cross had notified Bob of my arrival just two hours before my train was due. What if he had gone out for the day?

Bob was attending the University of Houston under the GI Bill, and after awhile I went to work for the Duncan Coffee Company. They were wonderful to me. My parents wanted to visit me, but only VIP's could travel at that time. Without my knowing, our company's transportation manager got my parents passage on the *America*, then the largest U.S. liner. They also helped me get a car, in very short supply right after the war.

Bob and I had only one daughter, but she has three beautiful children, so we're very fortunate. Cooking and housework aren't my forte, and I liked working in an office, so I carried on, eventually becoming a legal secretary until I retired. Since then I wonder how I ever had time to work. Volunteer jobs and especially TBPA have kept me busy. I've served as an officer in my branch, as Texas Area Secretary for twenty-four years and as Magazine and General Treasurer. At the 1974 New Orleans Convention I received my TBPA Life Membership. I treasure the friendships I've made.

After Bob retired from Tenneco, we built a vacation home that we enjoy, but we won't live there permanently. How could I give up my TBPA friends?

Nancy and Billy
1943: Friendly invasion of Essex

Nancy West from Roxwell, Essex lived in a modern house on Green Lane, a tranquil area "lined with horsechestnut trees, orchards and an abundance of primroses, paigles, violets and king cups." When she joined her groom, Billy Harrington, in rural Louisiana, she lived in a wooded area in a house without electricity or running water but plenty of hot weather, snakes, mosquitoes and dusty roads. Nancy faced the new challenges with pluck, hard work and youthful good spirits.

NANCY:

We met in August 1943 when the U.S. Army Air Force first came to England. Bases had been built almost in a ring around where I lived in Essex, and they were occupied by B-26 Marauder bombers. Billy was in the Medical Corp and stationed there. We met in the village pub, *Hare & Hounds*, where I was playing the piano for the usual sing-song. He made a date with my friend to meet outside the Village Hall the next day. I had a Brownies meeting at the Hall about the same time, and, when I came out, he was still waiting for her. I offered to show him where she lived, and we rode our bikes toward her house but didn't see her, so I took him for a ten-mile bike ride! Later, he accused me of taking him in the wrong direction to look for my friend.

We used to meet at the Jubilee Seat (in honor of King George V and Queen Mary) built around a sycamore tree, and a young people's hang-out. Mum soon met Billy, but my father didn't want me to go out with a Yank or bring one home. One day I bravely said, "Wouldn't you rather I brought him home than stay out with him?" So he relented.

A year later, we became engaged before Billy went to France. After VE-Day he came unexpectedly on seven-days leave and said "Let's get married." I was still under twenty-one, so we had to get dad to sign the papers given to us by the vicar. We found dad at the pub. Then we took the papers to the Bishop of Chelmsford and also to Westminster to get special permission for our marriage. Family and friends rallied around. A young widow whose husband had been killed in Dunkirk offered me her beautiful oyster satin wedding dress. I loved it! We even had six bridesmaids who already had dresses. Mum ordered flowers and a photographer. An aunt baked the wedding cake and neighbors iced it, peeled potatoes and so on. I know we had ox tongue for the wedding breakfast. Dad came up with the drinks. We were married 2 June 1945, and the bells of St. Michael's rang for the first wedding since 1939 when the war started. During the war, no church bells were to be rung except to warn of an impending invasion by Germany.

No time for a honeymoon as five of the seven-days leave had passed. We went to London for Billy's flight to Belgium, but it was

| I learned to cook strange things like okra, gumbo ... |

delayed for two days (fog). After that I didn't see him for another year, not until we met in Shreveport, Louisiana. When it was time for me to go to Tidworth, my family was great. No tears or recriminations, although my mother told me much later that dad had said, "That's the last we'll see of her!" But I took enough money with me to make a trip home, and I left on the train saying, "See you next year." At Tidworth we had to spend ten days waiting for repairs to the *Ericsson*. We finally sailed, and on 31 May 1946 we arrived in New York City.

After we landed, I went on to Shreveport where Billy met me. It was 90 degrees F, and I had a coat on my arm. Billy bought me a small suitcase for it, and we went to visit his father, stepmother and their sons who lived nearby. Then we went by train to live with the aunt and uncle who had raised Billy. They were Mama and Papa. We arrived after dark. There was no station, and the train stopped in a wooded area. A man met us in a pick-up truck and took us to a house where we were greeted on the front porch. I was given a glass of ice water, but everyone else drank from a bucket with a dipper. We were poor: Bill was a logger, and paydays were irregular. I learned to cook all the strange new things like okra, gumbo and turnip greens. I scrubbed clothes on a rub board. There was no electricity or running water. I took things in my stride, but sometimes I thought, "What am I doing here?"

People were friendly. I was impressed with canning vegetables by the bushel, quilting, shooting squirrels, going barefoot, snuff, and shotgun houses. I was homesick, and I kept my promise of seeing my parents "next year." We had a son, and we sailed to England for Christmas 1947--and stayed nine months. My parents visited us for Christmas the following year. We saw each other every year for the first six years. We always saved hard, did without things and spent all our money on the trip. We'd come back and start over again. Going home was our priority.

Things finally began to fall in place for us. In 1954 our second son was born, and we moved to the white frame house we'd hoped to have one day. After our third son was born, I didn't go home for thirteen years, but my family came often. I took a refresher course for typing, and since I'd attended "The Tech" in England for three years, I was considered a pro! On a tip from a neighbor about a job at the School Board Office, I applied there and was hired on the spot. Then in 1958 a State Civil Service job opened in the building where I was working. Bill applied and got the job. At last we had financial security.

Bill joined an Air Force Reserve unit in Natchitoches, and, when he retired, he was Chief Master Sergeant, the highest rank for an enlisted man. We went back to England for the 50th anniversary of the arrival of the Americans in East Anglia and a reunion of the 391st Bomb Group Association, "The Marauder Men."

I retired, as Executive Secretary, after thirty-one years at the local School Board. Our three sons are attorneys. We have eight grandchildren and consider ourselves blessed. Perhaps if we hadn't experienced those early years, we wouldn't now appreciate our good fortune so much.

1945: Outside Hendon Registry Office

**Newlyweds Doris Dark from Harrow, Middlesex
and Kenneth Riley, U.S. Army, from Atchison, Kansas.**

DORIS:

We were lucky to have this one wedding picture as we didn't have a camera. The taxi driver who was taking us to the Hendon Registry Office said, "What, no photos?" and he stopped at his house to get his camera. He even loaned me the bridal horseshoe for good luck. My blue wool wedding-dress material was bought on the black market. A far cry from the formal weddings of our own three daughters, way off in the future. Times were so different in war strained Britain.

My home was in London, and I had worked there until 1944. With the V-I buzz bombs coming over, my friend suggested we go for a (working) Farm Holiday. We went to Andover, Hampshire by train, and then lorries took us to the campsite where we slept in tents on straw mattresses. We had to work hard, digging potatoes out of a manure-filled haystack, and we were exhausted. When

> … "She'll spend all your money and she can't cook."

they asked for volunteers to work in the kitchen, we grabbed it. Also it gave us more spare time. My friend decided she would apply for work at the American Red Cross in nearby Tidworth. We both went, and they offered me a job too, as a secretary.

I met Kenneth in May 1945 just after VE-Day while I was still working for the ARC at Tidworth House. Ken had been wounded, and, after recovering in a Yoevil hospital, he'd been assigned to the U.S. Signal section in Tidworth. Sometimes I was a relief switchboard operator, and one day several GIs from the Signal section decided to come and see what the operators looked like. I happened to be on the board, and the rest is history, as they say!

When I took Ken home to London to meet my parents, my Mum gave him the third degree. By then we were planning to marry, but I was nineteen years old and needed their permission. My mother wasn't thrilled about it and told Ken that "She'll spend all your money and she can't cook." Ken's colonel had given the U.S. Army's permission and we sent the papers for my parents' approval. They hadn't had much formal education because of hard times when they were growing up, so when signing under "Parent" they signed "Mum and Dad." We had to start all over again.

We married in November 1945 and honeymooned at the Riviera Hotel in Torquay. It was a lovely place but full of uppity rich. For an extra shilling a day we had morning tea and breakfast served in bed. I often wondered what the maid thought of us as she brought breakfast on a silver tray, me in a wartime utility nightie and Ken in his GI underwear. One morning I ordered kippers. Ken had never seen a kipper before and picked it up by the tail and said with disgust, "What's this?"

Ken returned to America, and I followed in late March 1946, sailing on the *Holbrook*. Leaving London was hard. My family and friends came to see me off, and I've never seen so many people crying. When the train pulled out, we were all wondering whether we were doing the right thing. We went to Perham Downs in Tidworth, and it was like going home for me as I still had a lot of friends there at the Red Cross. I guess the thing that sticks out in my mind is the physical. We were given GI corduroy robes and told to strip and get in line. I kept getting out of line and going to

> ... Dad had warned me not to get off the train
> in case of being attacked by Indians.

the end until finally I had to grit my teeth to go through. There
was a U.S. Army doctor standing with his flashlight and chewing
gum. He shone the flashlight up and down, and then you were on
your way. We hoped we'd never see him again, but having a cup of
tea later on the doctor, in his charming American way, waved his
hand and said, "Hi girls!"

It took us nine days to come over. There were twenty-six of us
in a cabin, and I was so seasick I thought I would die. It was
wonderful to arrive in New York, 9th April. I thought the Statue of
Liberty very impressive, but the skyscrapers were not as white as I
had imagined. From the ship we went by bus to a railroad station.
Three of us went west to Kansas City. Before leaving London, Dad
had warned me not to get off the train in case of being attacked
by Indians. I thought the train lovely with the sleeping cars and
the amazing variety of food served in the dining-car. A nice lady
sat at our table and she was concerned about all the food
(calories) that we were eating. We were still hungry! We had a
layover in Chicago, and we stuck out like sore thumbs in our
tweed suits. The American girls looked slinky in their style of dress.

Ken met me in Kansas City, and after a couple of days there we
headed for Atchison, Kansas where his family lived. The people
were warm and friendly, and, as I was the only war bride around, I
was quite a novelty. Ken worked for the telephone company, but
in August he decided to make the army his career. I wasn't
thrilled, but I learned to love the life of living in different places
around the world. When Ken retired from the army, we settled in
Pacific Grove, California. We have three lovely daughters and five
grandchildren who are the joy of our life.

When I first came I was terribly homesick, and the summer
weather in Kansas was very hard to take. Lying on my bed I even
prayed for some good old English fog. One of my best friends
there was so homesick that she went back to England. I remember
my Mum told me, "You make your bed, you lie on it," and that old
saying has always stayed with me.

After fifty happy years, I think the taxi driver's wedding horseshoe did bring us luck.

4

REMEMBERING YESTERDAY

On His Majesty's Service

*Nothing moves an Englishman so much as the threat
of invasion, the reality unknown for a thousand years.
This was a time when all Britain worked . . . united as
never before. Men and women toiled at the lathes and
machines in the factories till they fell exhausted . . .
ordered home, while their places were occupied by
newcomers. Vast numbers of people were resolved to
conquer or die.*

Winston S. Churchill, "Alone," June 1940.

On 22 May, 1941, Parliament unanimously passed a bill giving the
Minister of Labour and National Service, Ernest Bevin, the power to
direct citizens to perform any service required for the nation's all-out war
effort. This resulted in young single women being conscripted into
National Service of some kind and found many others, including
housewives and older women, working outside the home. Britain urgently
needed the skills of all its people.

Of course, men had long since been mobilized into one of His
Majesty's armed forces, or into National Service as war workers, and now
more women would join them as they were called to serve in a variety of
ways. The first conscription of women was for the First Aid Nursing
Yeomanry Corps (FANY). Others went into one of the Women's
Auxiliary Services of the Army, Navy or Air Force; into the Land Army
helping farmers with their crops and livestock; or were trained to work in
factories that produced a whole gambit of much needed war materiél.

Those already engaged in work deemed vital to the war effort, or who
had careers considered essential to the nation, such as teachers and nurses,
were classified as being in "reserved occupations" and carried on as before.

Not surprisingly, many young girls now volunteered for active duty in the service of their choice, rather than wait until their age group was called up by the government.

The main Auxiliary Services for British women were these:

AIR FORCE: WAAF Women's Auxiliary Air Force.
ARMY: ATS Auxiliary Territorial Service.
LAND ARMY: Land girls helping farmers.
NAVY: WRNS (Wrens). Women's Royal Naval Service.
YEOMANRY CORPS: FANY First Aid and Nursing.

Many war brides have memories of the years they spent in His Majesty's Service, and Dorothy, Olive, Daphne, Audrey, June, Elizabeth and Annette are among them. These particular girls actively served from nineteen months to six years. Another young lady, Joyce, who expected to be conscripted into the ATS, got married two months after the 1944 D-Day invasion of Europe and was never called up. Clearly, the earlier 1940-41 national wartime emergency for recruiting young women was over.

In their own words, the recollections of these ladies continue the saga of the "GI Brides" as they tell about their courtship, marriage, arrival in America and their memories of those early years. They begin in 1942 when Dorothy Peers and Jim Crocus first met.

1943: June wedding
Jim in U.S. Army olive drab, Dorothy in Royal Air Force blue

Dorothy Peers from Wrexham, North Wales, joined the WAAF in 1941. She was twenty-one years old and served her country for three years when she was given a compassionate discharge. By that time she had married Jim Crocus, U.S. Army, from Glen Park, Indiana, and was expecting their first baby in October 1944.

DOROTHY:

It was in 1942 that I met Jim. I was stationed at Compton Basset, Wiltshire and training as a wireless operator. One evening the girls in our camp were invited to a dance by the U.S. Army stationed in nearby Devizes, and, though I didn't care for the Yanks, that's where I met my husband-to-be. I didn't intend to go to another dance, but when my friend wanted to go, I went too. There was Jim waiting for me.

Jim's group, the 344th Engineers, was sent to Algiers, but Jim became ill with pneumonia, so he was left behind. I visited him at the army hospital on weekends. We fell in love and on 3 January 1943 we became engaged. The U.S. Army required a three-months waiting period before giving permission to marry. We applied and signed papers, but they were lost--so we reapplied and those papers were also lost! Jim was transferred to HQ/ETOUSA, London and then Chester. He asked an Army chaplain for help in getting permission to marry, explaining that it had been five months since we'd first applied. The chaplain got us a marriage license.

We were married 26 June 1943 in the Christleton Methodist Church near Chester. Both the chaplain and the English reverend performed the ceremony, so that "it would be done right." My sister, older brother and wife and some of Jim's army friends attended the Saturday wedding. Jim was stationed for a year in Belfast, Northern Ireland--not far from the air base where I had been sent! We were able to spend most weekends together. Our first baby was expected in October 1944 and, not wanting to be stranded in Ireland when Jim left, I went back to live with my aunt in Leeswood, North Wales. Jim visited me there when our baby daughter arrived. He was now attached to SHAEF with the Allied Prisoner of War Recovery Unit and sent to Patton's headquarters in Luxembourg, then to Trier, Germany. When the war ended, Jim came to England, and we went to the American Consulate in Liverpool to register our daughter, so we could join Jim later on in America.

My daughter was seventeen months old when our travel orders arrived telling us to go to the Carlton Hotel in Bournemouth. It took three days for processing and a "physical." I remember the doctors coming around to check to see if we had any rashes. That was embarrassing. We sailed on 6 March 1946 on the *Queen Mary*.

Our neighbors were Croations and Serbs.

The American Red Cross was very helpful aboard ship. One dear lady wanted us to sing the national anthem of our new country, and we started off, but someone shouted, "What about England?" so we sang "There'll Always Be An England." Then of course we had to sing for the Scots, Welsh and Irish. We were only halfway across the ocean, and we hadn't given up our old country so soon. I made friends with a girl on the ship, and we had an awful time of it when both our babies were sick. From New York City we went on a train together but separated when I went to Indiana, and she went on to Washington state.

Jim met me at the Gary train station, and I was shocked at the shabbiness of the city as we drove south. When we reached the suburb of Glen Park, I was relieved to see how nice it was. Our neighbors were Croatians and Serbs. They were very nice and helped me adjust to my new life. We rented a small house before buying our first home in Glen Park. Our second daughter was born in January 1947, and she completed our family.

Jim worked while going to Northwestern University to get a degree in Business Administration. I was very lonely, but I knew we had to do this. I studied and became a U.S. citizen in 1950. Jim graduated in 1951, and was later employed by U.S. Steel.

My father-in-law was very generous and helped us immensely as our finances were not the best. I kept transferring the price of our food into British pounds and saying it was too high until Jim told me to forget about the pounds. There was a small grocery store nearby, and the grocer would stick extras (like butter or fruit) into my bag. As soon as I started to speak, people would look at me, and I felt embarrassed, but I got used it. One of my first impressions of America was the bigness of everything, and, when we took a trip out west, I was thrilled. This was the America I had read about and seen on films.

When my older daughter started school, she said things like "tomarto" and everyone laughed. She asked me why she spoke that way, and I told her she should speak the way the others spoke, but I never could. Our girls went on to college, and I found a good job at a credit bureau managed by an English lady. After she retired, I took over as manager. Later, I did volunteer hospital work and also helped teachers with special students. After getting her master's, our older daughter (who speaks Spanish and German) worked at embassies in Argentina and Austria. Our younger daughter and her husband have given us two fine grandsons. I've talked to them about Britain more than I did to my own children. In 1970 we visited Britain for the first time in twenty-five years. It was perfect. We also took a trip to Paris, Luxembourg and Trier, Germany, following in SHAEF's World War II footsteps.

We feel very happy with our lives--over fifty years of marriage-- and the way things turned out.

U.S. Army-British Navy wedding

13 October 1943, John Taylor & Olive Howe

When the war started in 1939, Olive Howe from Tadworth, Surrey was working for Coutts Bank in the Strand, London; but she soon volunteered for the Women's Royal Naval Service. Olive was stationed at Wavendon House, near Bletchley Park, and served for three years.

OLIVE:

I met Jack who came from Palisades Park, New Jersey, in 1942 at a Tea Dance given by the English Speaking Union in London. I was in the WRNS, and Jack was at the American Embassy. We knew one another for a year before we were married, and by then Jack was serving in the U.S. Army, 3118 Signal Service group.

My father wasn't too keen on my marriage, but we were in love and with everything else in order we were married 13 October

I made sure they knew they were Americans first.

1943 in Kingswood, Surrey. We spent our honeymoon in Shillingford Bridge, Oxfordshire, and then we lived in Putney for a while before Jack was sent to France.

Our oldest son was born in January 1945, but he was six months old before Jack saw him, prior to his return to the States. In March 1946 I received my travel orders and went to Tidworth for immigration processing. So many years have elapsed since then that I find it difficult to remember details. I know we sailed on a Swedish liner from Southampton, and the weather was rough. I wasn't seasick, but my young son ended up with a bad case of bronchitis. We landed 31 March 1946 in New York City, and Jack met us as the ship docked.

Our first home was in New Egypt, New Jersey. I had little knowledge of America when I arrived and think my education was sadly neglected in that respect. All of Jack's family and friends were extremely kind and friendly toward me. One of my first memories was of going to a Howard Johnson restaurant on the New Jersey Turnpike and having lamb chops. I hadn't had much food during the war, so everything tasted fine, except hamburgers. It took me a long time to eat one. Looking back I seem to have had food on my mind for over fifty years. It shows! Tea is still my favorite beverage--except for Scotch, of course.

We had three more sons, and, while I talked to them all about England, I made sure they knew they were Americans first. I also became an American citizen. Jack made the Army his career, and we lived overseas quite a bit, in the Philippines and other places. We had a tour of England in the 1950s, and that was really lovely. We also lived near Washington, D.C. off and on. I think the summer heat was one of the hardest things for me to handle.

Jack stayed in the Army for twenty-three years, and we didn't have a real home until he retired in 1964. I worked for many years in a bookshop, also as a tutor for adult literacy. We now live in Florida and our children and grandchildren often visit us.

We both love to travel and have visited almost all of the fifty states and Canada. We return to England to visit my sister and numerous relatives. Still, as we both love the country so much, we would go back even without family to visit. Cheers!

In the British Army

Daphne Fensom was living with her family in Cricklewood, London, when she left to join the ATS. Later, she met and married Hilton Scott, from Dellwood, Georgia who was serving in England with the U.S. Army Air Corps.
Going, in 1946, from a modern suburban home in London to a cabin-like dwelling in Georgia, without electricity, was a shock to Daphne. Like the pioneers of old, she gamely stuck it out.

DAPHNE:
During the war I served nineteen months in the ATS as a cook. I had been stationed at Marchwood, across from Southampton, at an anti-aircraft gun site. The first ATS girl to be killed in action was stationed there, on our AA (anti-aircraft) gun site. She was hit in the stomach by shrapnel. Our unit was disbanded, and I was sent as an assistant cook to a military hospital in Bedford.

One day a girl I worked with asked me to go to the fair in Bedford with her. She was dating a GI who was stationed at Sharnebrook, a supply depot for the U.S. Air Force at Thurleigh. He introduced me to his friend, Hilton. It was 6 August 1944; the day we met and fell in love. Just over three months later, on 25 November, we were married at the Mill Street Baptist Church in Bedford by the chaplain from the military hospital.

I borrowed a wedding dress and shoes. The shoes were too small, so I hobbled down the aisle on the arm of my father. He was an ex-marine and thought he had to march with precision to the organ music! We didn't have a honeymoon until the following March when Hilton got some leave. We went to Torquay, Devonshire, but it was so cold I ended up getting pneumonia.

Hilton returned to the States in August 1945, and I came in April 1946. I was at Tidworth for about three weeks, but that was so humiliating I'd like to forget it. I sailed on the *Ericsson*. We had 200 children and over 700 girls on board. About 100 of the girls were expectant mothers. It took us eleven days to cross, as we went down to the Azores and also lost the power of one engine.

We arrived in New York on Friday, 1 April, and since nobody worked on weekends, only the wives being met in New York were allowed off the boat. The rest of us had to wait until Monday.

> I cried another "Atlantic Ocean" of tears
> out there in the woods.

Finally, we landed, and I was put on a train going to Augusta, Georgia with two other girls. One girl was met in Augusta. The other girl and I went by Greyhound bus to Savannah where she was met. I then went on alone by bus to Swainsboro, Georgia, and my husband met me there.   He drove up US-1 to a small community called Dellwood. There he turned off on a path through the woods to a "house" by the railroad tracks of the Wadley Southern line.

I was used to living in N.W. London, and here I was in a dwelling place that wasn't sealed, with a wood stove and only kerosene lamps. I cried another "Atlantic ocean" of tears out there in the woods. I know I was homesick for five years before I really began to adjust.

After twenty years I went home for my first visit. We have eight children, all happily married and doing very well, and twenty healthy grandchildren. I have a husband who loves me very much and never lied to me about his grand house or luxury living. He has supported me in every way possible and has spoiled me with his generosity. I wouldn't change places with anyone I know.

We celebrated our 50th wedding anniversary together. Life has not been easy, but we have been richly blessed.

* * * * *

We have no wartime photograph of Daphne or Hilton. They lost every-thing in 1953 when a tornado hit their home in Warner Robins, Georgia.

Daphne died two years after their 50th anniversary. At the funeral service, Eileen, one of Daphne's eight children, spoke of her mother's selfless love in serving others. The Salvation Army (founded in London) always played an important role in Daphne's life. She was a "special woman" who gave much of herself and whose influence will go on.

Six years in the WAAF

Audrey Firkin, from Birmingham, volunteered for service with the Royal Air Force in 1939, and served for the duration. As a war bride, Audrey was eligible to sail to America under the U.S. Army's Transportation plan, but she chose to make her own arrangements.

AUDREY:

Anthony Stern came from New York, and I met him in June 1944 at an American Red Cross Club in Bayswater, London. I was then twenty-nine years old, lived in Sloan Street and served as a WAAF staff officer with the Ministry of Aircraft Production. Anthony was twenty-five years old and was with the U.S. Army, G-2 Counter Intelligence, attached to the British Permit Office.

We were immediately attracted to one another, and six months after we met we were married. Some members of my family tried to dissuade me, but our wedding took place on 23 December 1944 at St. Saviour's Church, Walton Street, London. We spent our honeymoon in Torquay, Devon and then had a flat at 167 Park West, Edgeware Road in London. This photo of us was taken on the roof of our building--not a sought after location at the time when Hitler's "doodle bugs" were coming over!

London 1944: Audrey & Tony Stern

> We staged a protest and were taken ashore on a tender,
> but our luggage remained on the ship.

When the war was over, my husband returned to the States, and I started to make my own arrangements for transportation to America.

After paying my own fare, I sailed on 12 April 1946 from Cardiff, Wales on a Liberty ship, the *James Bennett Moore*. There were only seven other passengers aboard the small cargo vessel, none of them war brides. We had excellent food the first week; then we went on emergency rations since the crew wished to delay the voyage so as to arrive in New York City on a weekend. But when we finally arrived there, no docking space was available. We staged a protest and were taken ashore on a tender, but our luggage remained on the ship. We landed, after a two week's voyage, and my husband was there waiting to meet me.

Before coming to the U.S. I already had a picture of what it was like because during the last two years of the war I had been stationed near American camps. I found Americans interesting and stimulating, though not quite open-minded.

At first we lived in New York City. Two years later we moved to Albertson, Long Island where our three children were born. I've always talked to them and to friends about Britain. Our family has not only visited England many times, but English relatives are frequent visitors over here. I became an American citizen in 1962. Much of New York City and its environs are Anglo-American as far as social life is concerned. Also, my husband was a United Nations employee, so we tended to mix with groups of different nationalities, including many English.

We lived in Briarcliff, New York for over forty years. I worked for fifteen years as a Business Administrator for adjoining school districts, and retired in 1982. I continued to be active in several service organizations such as the League of Women Voters, the Ossining Food Pantry, local church, garden and book clubs, art and the theatre. I belong to the RAF Association, but I don't know any other war brides.

Our family has grown and it now includes three grandchildren. Recently we moved to California. Life in America has been good, but the hardest thing to get used to was the lack of the institution of "afternoon tea!"

1944: June in the WAAF

**June volunteered when she was sixteen years old
and served for three years.**

June Marston, from Totton, near Southampton, Hampshire was serving in the Women's Auxiliary Air Force when she met William (Bill) Harris, a sailor in the U.S. Navy from Alabama. In spite of her mother's objections that "Alabama is too far to go," that's where June went after the war when she joined Bill in America. Texas came later.

JUNE:

In 1944, when Bill was in the U.S. Navy and I was in the WAAF, we met at a dance in Cardiff. Except that each of us was with someone else. I had hoped to go to an officer's dance at Cardiff Castle the next night, but Bill kept cutting in until the officer went away--no dance at the castle for me. I was told later that when Bill returned to his ship he announced that he intended to marry me!

We had a couple of dates before Bill's ship pulled out. I was posted to Yorkshire. After misplacing his letter, I felt sure that "that was that," but fate thought otherwise. Bill's ship went to Southampton, and he was soon on my parent's doorstep; and I was posted back to Andover only seventeen miles away!

I was able to get home and interpret such things as "Hampshire Hog" and "Alabama Red Neck" for them. Before long we got engaged. There wasn't much red tape, but I did have to meet Bill's captain. So did Gladys, a nurse, who was dating Bill's friend Blackie. It was all arranged, and, with some apprehension, we were picked up on the quay by a PT (patrol torpedo) boat, with disapproving looks by dowager ladies walking their dogs. After a thrilling ride down Southampton Water we reached the LST (landing ship, tank) where we were confronted by a rope ladder. We were both in uniform, and there was no way we would climb that swaying rope in tight skirts, so the bow of the ship was lowered (used for landing tanks). Up we went through the bowels of the ship to be given a royal reception that Gladys and I relive to this day. It was just before Christmas, and Bill's friends shared their packages from home with us--sweets, gum and so on, that we later shared with our families. And then, dinner with the Captain! We hadn't seen such food in ages.

Bill was impressed too, because an enlisted man rarely dines with the Captain. Not only did Captain Blalock approve our marriage but he wrote to Bill's mother and assigned Bill to Shore Duty. After my Mum's initial objection and a six month's engagement, we were allowed to plan our wedding. It was quite lavish for the times. The banns were called the requisite three times; the American Red Cross lent me a beautiful white gown, and each of my four bridesmaids produced a pastel-colored dress, each a different style. We coordinated the colors with bouquets and head-dresses that we made ourselves. They looked like a lovely bunch of spring flowers.

> Bill signed for me at the Navy table and with both
> of us in tow went to the Army table to sign for Glad.

We were married Wednesday, 7 March 1945 at Eling St. Mary,
our local 12th-century church. My grandma, a bit of a snob,
insisted that only common people married on Saturdays. Grandma
provided a wedding breakfast, and later we danced to a small band
in the village hall. My dad had a taxi business, and he provided a
shiny limousine trimmed with the traditional wide satin bridal
ribbons. Then it was a train journey to Torquay: sand, sunshine
and love.

I was still in the WAAF, but my sympathetic C.O. had me posted
to Romsey, and I was allowed to billet at my own home, just five
miles away. So Bill and I stayed close until I was demobbed, and he
was shipped back to the U.S. later that year.

Early in 1946 I campaigned successfully for Gladys and me to
sail together on the *Queen Mary's* first "bride" voyage. (No, Glad
didn't marry Blackie but instead a Yank from Minnesota). It was in
February, and after a few days at Tidworth Camp we endured a
rough crossing but recovered sufficiently to thrill at the sight of
the Statue of Liberty. Then we landed in New York City.

Army vehicles took us to the Armory where Bill was waiting.
Glad's husband, Bob, had wired Bill for him to meet her and to
put her on a plane to Minneapolis. This caused a commotion. Bill
signed for me at the Navy table and with both of us in tow went
to the Army table to sign for Glad. Loud cries of "only one per
man, fella" followed us until Bill produced the wire from Bob.
What a laugh!

Glad got her flight all right, and Bill and I took the train to
Alabama. I was introduced to fried chicken and assured that it was
OK to eat it with my fingers. I met many interesting people and
will never forget the friendly conductor who woke me from a nap
with a command to "say something!" Also intrigued by my accent
was the manager of the local A&P, and my mother-in-law was soon
insisting on my grocery shopping with her because, if I would just
say "tin of tomatoes," then Mr. Fuller would ply us with items that
were in short supply (they called it rationing--Ha!).

I settled down pretty well, considering my tender age, and very
soon had gathered together a group of GI brides. Later some of

them joined TBPA, but that was after we had moved to Texas, and I had helped form the Texas Area. How we survived the heat with no air conditioning and the terrifying electric storms, I'll never know, but our TBPA group met frequently and supported each other. I have served many years as the National Travel Counselor. In 1986 I was honored to be made a Life Member of TBPA. Our lovely family now includes a great-grandchild.

Bill was always "at my side" until, sadly, after nearly forty-nine years of happy marriage, he died, following a long illness.

* * * * *

After Bill's death, June's health declined and she died suddenly in 1995. Her daughters, Jennifer and Janet, carry on June's delightful spirit and traditions with their growing families. They also remain active in TBPA, the British Heritage Society that June had enjoyed and worked so hard for.

On His Majesty's Service in the Royal Navy

**Elizabeth with her hair "off the collar in the roll
we wore in those days. Tidy anyway!"**

Elizabeth Spirit from Great Barrow, Cheshire, worked at the Chester Public Library after leaving secondary school. In 1943, she volunteered for the WRNS and served for two years.

ELIZABETH:

When I met John Quinn, from St. Louis, Missouri, I had no intention of getting involved with a GI. It was March 1944, and I was stationed near London. We met at a dance at a WVS (Women's Voluntary Service) Canteen in Ruislip, Middlesex. John was waiting for a girl in the WAAF, but he danced with me and remarked that the crowded place reminded him of a rat race back home. "Oh! Good Heavens, man, you don't race rats in America, do you?" I remarked, being sarcastic. He roared with laughter, and the whole room wanted to know the joke. Served me right! That was the beginning of our romance. I was nineteen years old and John was twenty-two years old. Fifteen months later we were married.

My father did not approve of me marrying a Yank until he met John. Once my parents gave their approval, the U.S. military did too. We were married 18 June 1945 by special license at my parish church in Great Barrow, near Chester. I was still in the WRNS and stayed in until the war with Japan was over, and then returned to live with my parents. By then I was pregnant, and John was on his way home to St. Louis, Missouri. I hoped to follow soon.

Early in March 1946, when I was about six-months pregnant, I received my U.S. Army travel order and was sent to Tidworth for processing. After some delays we were put aboard the *E.B. Alexander*. I was seasick and didn't eat much--the tin trays clanging in the mess and queuing up for food was too much. Being pregnant I got milk from the baby formula area. The water tasted of chlorine, so it was hard to drink. I put a candy in my mouth to take the taste away. Water for a cup of tea was drawn from the faucet, so there wasn't a good cup of HOT tea aboard ship. The voyage took nine days, and we had no entertainment that I remember. During the voyage, one of the crew tried to molest one of the girls, so the police came aboard when we reached New York and took the crewman off.

We arrived in New York around 28 March 1946. We were young, and everyone was apprehensive about life ahead in America. I remember seeing the bright colored taxis as we sat on the ship in the harbor. We had help and kind words from some ladies at dockside and from the bus driver who took us from the dock to the train at Pennsylvania Station. Another girl, Mildred Ritter, traveled with me to St. Louis, and we formed a lasting friendship. John was there to meet me at Union Station. As we

... "Oh, your wife is the lady who speaks broken English?"

drove through mid-town St. Louis, I was appalled by the slums (now all cleared) where black people lived.

My husband's family was very kind and made me welcome. I had read a few books about America, and I knew it would be a different life. The resentment I got from some people seemed to be because I spoke "different"--always known as "That English lady!" One lady talking to my husband in the early years said, "Oh, your wife is the lady who speaks broken English?" John said, "It's the King's English!"

Eating chicken with fingers was a new custom to me, and also learning to like corn-on-cob (chicken food). I missed not having the sea nearby, or a woods or country lane to walk in. I hadn't reckoned on the summer heat, the great distances and the poor public transportation when I was used to traveling in England alone and not being afraid. I missed seeing my family and friends.

Our son was born July 2, 1946 just three months after my arrival in the states. My first year was spent traveling with my husband in his telephone job. We would be away a week or more, staying in small town motels. It was hard with a baby. The other wives had no children and went off shopping and to movies, but I learned to make my own friends.

In 1947 we bought a house in St. Louis County, Missouri. I went to night school at Washington University for my library certificate and worked at the university's reference library.

John was recalled to service during the Korean War and went to Japan. I found it very hard on my own, so I rented out our house and went back to England for five months. That settled me to living in the U.S. on my return from the trip, and in December 1951, I became a citizen.

Today, John and I are both retired. We are proud of our lovely grandchildren. I still drink tea and like mince pies at Christmas and First Footing at New Year's. We both enjoy going to the 3118th Signal Service Veterans annual reunions.

When I was very young and talked back to my parents, I used to say, "All right, you'll be sorry when I go to live in America"--thinking when I said it, that it was such a long way away. And yet, here I am. Was it ESP?

1943: Annette Bridges in the Land Army

Annette (Beryl) Bridges lived in Langley, Birmingham, where her widowed mother ran a boarding house for college students and teachers. When Annette was only sixteen years old, she used her mother's name and joined the Land Army. She served for four years, most of it working hard on a dairy farm in The Malverns, Worcestershire.

Later, when living in Missouri she milked cows by lantern light--just like the Land Army. In Texas she worked even harder but not on a farm.

ANNETTE:

I joined the Land Army in 1940. It was a bad year for Britain after the fall of France and the heroic Dunkirk evacuation. Thousands of wounded men were loaded onto special trains, and every day they passed through the fields where I was working. Later, I was stationed on a dairy farm in The Malverns, Worcestershire.

One Saturday afternoon in 1944, I went to Great Malvern to go to the pictures. I looked to see what was on when a Yank, who was also looking, spoke to me. He was Melvin Langenberg, U.S. Army, from Owensville, Missouri, stationed with the 55th General Hospital in Malvern. He asked me to go to the show with him, and I did. We dated for several months, and then he was sent to Nancy, France. Before he left, he asked me if I would be the mother of his children, and at the age of twenty, I said "Yes!"

Soon after the end of the war, I received a telegram from Melvin saying he'd be with me in four days time for our marriage. It was a rush, and I had to borrow everything, but I was ready. We were married 22 September 1945 at Oldbury Parish Church, near Birmingham. We had a fairly large wedding and reception and went to Stratford-upon-Avon for our honeymoon. His best man told the Swan's Nest hotel that we wanted twin beds. That's what we got! We had a wonderful time.

The following May 1946, I left home to join Melvin in the States, where he'd just been discharged. At Tidworth we got bumped from the *Queen Mary* by Canadian girls who had higher priority. We sailed on the *Thomas Barry*, a troop ship. The food was really great. I was three months pregnant, and I didn't miss a meal; didn't keep one down either. One of the girls became very ill on the voyage, and we stopped off the coast of Newfoundland to pick up an iron lung for her. In New York it was wonderful to see the Statue of Liberty, especially since I'd been sick all the way.

I took a train from New York City to St. Louis, Missouri, where Melvin, handsome in civilian clothes, met me. It was dark outside, and there were thousands of fireflies. The first time I had seen bugs with tail-lights--a sparkling fairyland!

At first we lived on a farm with Melvin's parents in Owensville, Missouri. Funny, we were fighting the Germans, and I married a man of German background. They spoke a lot of German around the house, and their church services were in German.

> . . . I lost the love of my life
> after twenty-three years of marriage.

After our first son was born in 1946, on "Guy Fawkes" fireworks day, the 5th of November, we moved to Columbia and then Montgomery City where Melvin worked as a journalist. When the baby was a year old, I went back to England to help my mother sell everything, so she could move to America with me. In 1952 I became a U.S. citizen. Our lovely family grew, and eventually Melvin and I had three sons and a daughter. By then we were living in Victoria, Texas, and both of us worked for the local *Advocate* newspaper.

We started on a new venture in Victoria when we bought three dry-cleaning plants, a commercial laundry and "washaterias" in three large apartment complexes. Melvin worked two jobs, and I was in charge of the dry-cleaning and laundry business, with the help of managers for each place. We both worked very hard to get these businesses going well for our retirement. Then in 1967, Valentine's Day, we were totally torn apart when Melvin had acute heart failure and was told he'd never work again.

On 9 January 1968, I lost the love of my life after twenty-three years of marriage. He was only forty-five years old when he died. My oldest son, in the Air Force, received a hardship discharge so that he could help me with the businesses, but it proved to be too much without my hubby--and too expensive hiring everything done that I couldn't do. I went bankrupt.

I made a fresh start and found a newspaper job with the *Conroe Courier*, in Texas. In 1972, I met Anthony Grawey, an airplane mechanic who was divorced with one son. Four years after I lost Melvin, I married Anthony, whose background is French. The years have flown by and we've already celebrated our twenty-fifth wedding anniversary.

When I visited England in 1976, I saw my brother for the first time in nearly thirty years. Now I go often, but when my brother died I felt I had wasted all those years without a visit to him. Now it's too late. I will always love England and go back for visits as long as I am able.

I married two super guys, one a Yankee and one a Rebel. Thankfully, I have a wonderful family, and we are all real close.

1944: Joyce Howlett & James Cubley

Helen Joyce Howlett was living at home in Aylsham, Norfolk, with her family, ready and waiting to be called for duty in the Army ATS, when in April 1944, she met a soldier from Lane, Oklahoma. Meantime, the conscription of young British girls for national service diminished after the successful Allied invasion of mainland Europe. Joyce never joined the army. Instead, her life began to steer in an entirely different direction.

JOYCE:

James Cubley was in the U.S. Army Air Force stationed at Deopham Green, Norfolk. He and other GIs used to ride their bicycles to Hingham when off duty, and leave their bikes at my friend's house for safekeeping. This is where I met James in April, about six weeks before D-Day. It was love at first sight! We soon planned to get married.

| The vastness of the country was overwhelming. |

My parents tried to discourage me, and my sister, married to an RAF officer, also tried to dissuade me. They didn't like the idea of me going so far away from home. I was interviewed by a U.S. chaplain, and we had no difficulty getting approval for our marriage. Five months after we met, we were married on 16 August 1944 at St. Michael's Church, in Aylsham, Norfolk.

After that we were able to be together until the war ended and James returned to the States. I was pregnant by then, and in March 1946 our first daughter was born. Our daughter didn't have a passport, which created problems later in the U.S.A. Officials helped us with specific problems, but being timid I avoided them as much as possible.

In June 1946 we were sent to Tidworth by the U.S. Army. The American Red Cross gave us cookbooks and held talks about America, but we didn't see them on board ship. When we set sail on the *Ericsson* from Southampton, there was a band playing and lots of GI brides' relatives waving good-bye on the dock. We were under way, but, before we got out of sight of land, there was a problem with the ship, and we were towed back to harbor. What an anticlimax! We couldn't leave the ship, however, and stayed in dock several days for repairs. Finally, we set sail again on June 20th.

I shared a cabin with another girl but I rarely saw her because her baby became ill and was put in sickbay. I stayed busy on the voyage taking care of my baby. One day I discovered that someone had gone through my cases and taken what they wanted. That was very upsetting. When we arrived in New York City there was a train strike on so James drove 900 miles from Amarillo, Texas, where he was living, to meet us at the dock. There was a photographer taking photos of couples meeting--wish I knew where those pictures are now. Then James drove us nearly non-stop from New York to Texas.

I knew very little about America or what to expect. The vastness of the country was overwhelming. My husband's family made me very welcome and tried to make me feel at home. Sundays and special occasions we were always invited out for dinner to their houses, and invariably I threw up, not being used to the rich food.

> ... coming to America and being so far from my family
> made me a self-reliant person in many ways.

Some of the women I met were rude and made nasty remarks about foreigners stealing their boys. I spent the first year wanting to go home. My husband was very patient with me until one day he presented me with a ticket home. After that I decided to make a bigger effort to adjust, and did. It really was hard though; the climate in Texas was so different; the heat, blowing sand and insects bothered me tremendously. I wasn't a homemaker and didn't know much about keeping house and cooking, but I soon learned.

Our second daughter was born in 1950, and five years later our son arrived. I became a citizen in 1951. Being a wife and mother was a full time job while the children were young, but later I worked as a pharmacy assistant for twenty years. We've lived in Novato, California since 1957 and have lots of friends in town. We enjoy a good game of bridge and also traveling across country with our 5th-wheel trailer. Our children and grand-children live close by. They've always been interested in British traditions and also in seeing my relatives who visit us from England. We go back there quite often too.

Looking back, coming to America and being so far from my family made me a self-reliant person in many ways. James and I feel fortunate that we share such a happy and satisfying life together.

WORLD WAR II GROOMS

Cary Grant played the ultimate war groom when he appeared on the silver screen in a humorous movie called *I Was a Male War Bride*. As a handsome French officer married to an American WAC (Women's Army Corps) lieutenant, he wants to sail to New York on a ship carrying foreign-born GI Brides. He doesn't appear to fit in, of course, but he steadfastly tells impatient officials that he is eligible to sail because he is an "alien spouse of female military personnel." The U.S. military are perplexed at this outlandish statement and want nothing to do with him. Frustrated, Cary Grant finally resorts to dressing up as a war bride and boards the ship! Still, Hollywood got it right in one respect. America's World War II foreign war grooms were rare, but they were there. An American servicewoman who was sent overseas during the war was just as susceptible to falling in love "over there" as was GI Joe.

After Public Law 271 was passed by the United States Congress, 28 December 1945, any alien spouse of an "honorable" member (or former member) of the U.S. armed forces was eligible to enter America as a nonquota immigrant. Thousands of war brides were clamoring for ships when, early in 1946, the *War Brides Operation* spun into action. Thus the big U.S. Army transit center at Perham Down near Tidworth, and the Carlton Hotel in Bournemouth, opened and were ready to receive these girls, some with babies or young children. So it was a surprise when a "male war bride" turned up for processing before sailing to America.

Actually, there were 322 war grooms of female U.S. military personnel who entered the States during the three-year life of this law. Like the war brides, they came from over thirty different countries scattered all over the world. There were between three and twenty men from each of the following nations: Australia, New Zealand, France, the Netherlands, Belgium, Norway, Poland, Greece, Spain, Italy, the USSR and parts of Asia; forty-three hailed from Canada, and sixty came from Great Britain.

John Spencer was one of those British men who went to Tidworth as a war groom and then, unlike Cary Grant in the movie, had no trouble boarding a ship with the GI brides and sailing to America.

1945: Blanch (Mickey) Mason and John W. Spencer

Outside the old Anglican Church in Viareggio, Italy

JOHN:

When the war started I was living in Washington, County Durham (now Tyne & Wear) in the north of England. Yes, the old town where George Washington's ancestors lived--although my family arrived there long after the Washington family had left! I was doing substitute teaching for the Durham County Education Commission, after going to Leeds University. In 1939 I volunteered for the British Army and was soon sent to Officer Training with the Royal Corps of Signals. I went overseas in 1942 with the British 1st Army.

I was with the Army Air Support Control, Signal Section, and after the invasion of Salerno, Italy, I was attached to the 5th U.S. Army Headquarters in Florence. It was mid-1944 when Mickey and I met on a blind date. She was a U.S. Army nurse from Troy, Pennsylvania, with the 24th General Hospital which was just across the road from our HQ. An American officer I knew had asked my cooperation with a blind date. Mickey and I got along very well, and we managed to continue to meet one another, even after I had moved north as the war operations progressed.

At the end of hostilities in Europe, May 1945, Mickey told me that the 24th Hospital was scheduled to go to the Far East. We decided to get married as soon as possible. There was no difficulty in "getting permission" although I was interviewed by a U.S. chaplain. Ten months after we met, we were married on 20 June 1945 by an American Lutheran chaplain in an Anglican Church in Viareggio, Italy. Mickey wore a lovely white wedding dress, and after the ceremony we had a large reception at the Casino in town. We went to Venice for our honeymoon. After our marriage Mickey was attached to several hospitals in Austria and again in Italy, but we got together frequently until Mickey went back to the States.

I returned to England in June 1946 where, after six years in the army, I received my discharge and saw my family again. My younger brother had joined the Royal Air Force, and in 1944 he was sent to Canada for Flight Training. He died there in a flying accident. He was only nineteen years old. Having lost one son, my mother wasn't pleased to see me leaving the country again. Meanwhile, Mickey was applying for my transportation to America, and in late August my travel papers from the U.S. Army arrived.

> We had to have a physical examination before we
> sailed, and at first we queued up with the brides ...

I must say that the people at Tidworth were a little nonplussed when they saw me, but it was no problem for me. In fact, there was another bridegroom there. The two of us were given a dormitory complete with twenty-four beds. This plus two hostesses who were assigned to our quarters, as was usual with each dormitory. You can imagine that we had a lot of laughs! Once we even trooped off to the pictures in the nearby town. We had to have a physical examination before we sailed, and at first we queued up with the brides at the appointed time until we were told to go to another room. Finally, after a week's delay, we sailed on the *President Tyler* from Southampton. There were 248 GI brides and children, two bridegrooms and some returning Red Cross workers on the ship. The trip got a little rough, and the dining room was somewhat deserted at times.

We arrived 6 September 1946 and landed on Staten Island, New York. Mickey was on the dock waiting for me. We went to Troy, Pennsylvania and shared a home with Mickey's sister and family. I was welcomed by all the relatives. As I'm very adaptable, I had no problems. I'd learned quite a bit about America during those three years I was attached to the U.S. Army in Europe.

We stayed in Troy until 1947 when Mickey and I moved to Silver Spring, Maryland. I started to teach at the Bullis School there, a private preparatory school, and taught Mathematics and Science to students in the Upper and Middle Schools. In August 1951 I became an American citizen.

My mother and dad came out to see us. My mother was very anxious to go to Ottawa to visit my young brother's grave. We had friends who lived up there, so we drove to Canada and stayed with them while visiting the cemetery. I think my mother felt more at peace after seeing where my brother was buried. When we got back to Maryland, however, she said she'd like to see Toronto. She didn't realize it was 500 miles away, and we'd just come back from Canada!

I retired from Bullis School in 1981, but I still maintain my association with the school and help out there occasionally. For some years we were interested in breeding and showing bulldogs and continued this until about 1987. However, I maintain my interest in dog shows as a steward; sort of a judge's administrative assistant in the ring.

Mickey passed away in 1990 after a stroke and a long period in a nursing home, and she is buried in Arlington National Cemetery near Washington, D.C. Now, I live by myself in the house we built together back in 1959.

WAR BRIDES TO CANADA

A valued member of the British Commonwealth of Nations, the Dominion of Canada declared war on Germany, 10 September 1939, only a week after Great Britain's declaration. Over 500,000 Canadians served overseas for the next six years in either the Royal Canadian Army, Air Force or Navy until the Allied victory was won. Finally, with the war over, the service men would soon be going home, and for those Canadians who had fallen in love and married while overseas it meant that they would be "bringing home" war brides. By the end of 1946, a total of 47,783 war brides and nearly 22,000 children had arrived in Canada from Britain, Holland, Belgium, France and elsewhere. Many Canadians had been stationed in the British Isles for more than two years, and, like the Yanks, most of their wartime marriages abroad took place there. So, while 70,000 British brides sailed to the United States, 45,000 of their "sisters" headed for Canada.

The Canadians had been as friendly and unceremonious as the Yanks in their quest to meet the local girls, but, as with the U.S. Army, Canadian military authorities disapproved of couples getting engaged or married.

The topic was addressed in: *Canadian Army Routine Order No. 788; Permission to Marry, North West Europe.*

This order instructed Commanding Officers to try to dissuade young men from marriage in foreign lands and, with help by the chaplain, to protect them from "improvidence and impetuosity." The Commanding Officer could refuse to give his consent if he was "not satisfied that a reasonable base for a happy marriage existed." Canadian war brides, however, faced less red tape than the American GI brides encountered, as the CO's permission was the only military requirement. Also, marriage at that time to a Canadian national automatically conferred citizenship on the bride. (After 1 January 1947, anyone not born in Canada had to apply for citizenship.)

All the necessary medical tests and immigration documents required by the Canadian war brides as they prepared to leave their homeland were dealt with on a personal basis. Transportation was assigned by the Department of National Defence, and the Canadian Wives Bureau provided support. The girls did not have to spend several days in a processing center (like Tidworth) before boarding a ship. They usually left home on the appointed date, traveled to a meeting point, usually in London, where they stayed overnight in hostels or hotels. Some girls went directly to the seaport and sailed within a day. Like the GI brides, they were given free rail and transatlantic transportation, meals and medical care from their parents' homes to their husbands' places of residence overseas.

Once they reached their final destinations in Canada, some of the girls were taken aback by the primitive conditions they found. A few were disappointed by the boastful exaggerations of what to expect. Nevertheless, most of the war brides stayed, worked hard and adjusted nicely to family life in the New World. Canada is now their home.

A Scottish girl, Mary, and an English girl, Daphne, from the London area tell about meeting and marrying Canadian soldiers.

1943: Mary Boyle in St. James Park, London

Mary Boyle lived with her widowed mother in Glasgow, Scotland and worked as an invoice typist for Bayne & Duckett. In June 1941, she volunteered for the WAAF and served until December 1944.

MARY:

I was twenty-one years old and in the WAAF when I met John Leon from Lethbridge, Alberta, at the Locarno Dance Hall in Glasgow. It was December 1942, and he was on his first leave from Colchester where he was stationed. Johnny was twenty-five years old and attached to the 112th Artillery Regiment, Royal Canadian Army. I was a WAAF teleprinter operator, stationed in Harrogate until I got a compassionate posting closer to my home in Glasgow. Sadly, my mother had received a telegram stating that my brother Tom, a Royal Air Force observer (navigator and bomb aimer) was killed. He had been shot down the night of August 31st 1941 in Belgium, after a bombing raid over Essen, and four of the crew of five were killed.

> Canadian citizenship was automatic
> for me the day I married Johnny.

After Johnny and I met, we wrote often, and he came to see me on his next leave. We got engaged. He applied to his Commanding Officer for permission to get married, and it was granted. Canadian citizenship was automatic for me the day I married Johnny. Six months after we met, we were married, 10 June 1943, at St. Peter's Roman Catholic Church in Glasgow. We went to Dunoon for our honeymoon, a small seaside resort down the River Clyde. At that time the place was crowded with sailors.

Just before our marriage I had been posted to Harrow-on-the-Hill, near the outskirts of London, and I spent eighteen months there before going to Prestwick, my last posting. Any time Johnny and I had leave, we always went to my mother's house in Glasgow. I left the service in December 1944 when I became pregnant. Looking back, I really enjoyed the WAAF once I got over my homesickness. There were lots of air-raids, but we were never bombed out. My family didn't want me to leave and go to Canada, but I applied for transportation, and in March 1945 I received my travel orders. I was five-months pregnant then. The war was still being fought, and security was extremely tight. We had to stay overnight in Glasgow at a place they called the "Poor House," so that nobody would know when we were leaving.

On 7 March 1945 we boarded the *Aquitania* and sailed from Greenock. I can't remember how many young brides and children were on the ship. We made friends with some, but others had their husbands on board, so they didn't mix with us. I enjoyed the food--but it came up afterwards! We played cards a lot. I was annoyed because, being pregnant, I was supposed to have a lower bunk, but one girl with a child wouldn't let me have it. They slept there and I had to climb to the upper bunk.

We arrived in Halifax, Nova Scotia on 14 March 1945, and then I went on to Alberta. A Red Cross lady helped me in the train going across Canada. She gave me her card and said that I should get in touch with her if I ever wanted to go home. I still have the card. When we reached Lethbridge station, I got off and found my mother-in-law and ladies from the Legion all waiting to meet me. I had arrived in Canada three weeks before my husband came home

> **I was presented with**
> **the coveted Canadian Forces Decoration. . . .**

and I knew I wasn't welcome at that time. I soon felt ready to go back to Scotland!

Some friends of my husband did more for me than anyone. When my husband arrived in Calgary, he had a month's leave, so we traveled around and visited his relatives in different cities. After his holiday he applied at the Alberta Government Telephones and got a job right away.

We had our own apartment in Lethbridge, and on 8 July 1945 the child that I was carrying when I arrived was stillborn. What a tragedy that was. I wished I had never come to Canada but stayed in Glasgow to have the baby. My second child was born in June 1947, Catherine Mary Isabel. Isabel was my mother's name, and she came to Canada for the baby's birth and stayed for nine months. Three years later our son Donald was born. We took the family home several times, also to France, Belgium, Holland and Ireland, so they saw different countries and met their aunties and uncles.

My husband's job took us to several places in Alberta and then back to Lethbridge where we had our present home built. I got a job and worked for the 18th Field Artillery Regiment, RCA. Later, when the regular army sergeant was transferred to Germany, I filled in and worked as an administrator until a replacement could be found. At that time I went on permanent call-out (active service). My job finished in 1962. I was presented with the coveted Canadian Forces Decoration by Brigadier Leech, marking twelve years of meritorious service. It was the first C.D. presented here to a member of the Canadian Women's Army Corps.

Johnny retired after thirty-five years, and we keep busy with volunteer jobs, trips and clubs. I serve as secretary on the Provincial Board of the Alberta War Brides Association. Johnny's wartime Battery formed an Association, and we're both active in that. We're proud of our family. Our grandson, Greg, graduated from the University of Lethbridge, and another grandson, Bryan, received a football scholarship at Calgary University. He just loves sports, and we love to cheer him on. We've already celebrated our 50th Golden wedding anniversary. How the years have gone by!

1946: Lloyd Raven and Daphne Butcher
outside of St. John's Church, Wembley

Daphne Butcher lived in Wembley, Middlesex, and worked as a secretary for the Society of Motor Manufacturers at Hyde Park Corner, London. Since the company made war vehicles, Daphne was "exempt" from being conscripted for another wartime occupation.

DAPHNE:

Lloyd Raven from Toronto, Canada and I met in August 1945 at the end of World War II. I was at the seaside on holiday in Folkestone, Kent with my mother and aunt. We were in a quaint old pub one day, and sitting at the next table were three Canadian servicemen. We all got into conversation with them and found out that they had just returned from the Continent. One of them, Lloyd, was being sent to London while waiting to go back to Canada, and he asked to see me again. I agreed and gave him my address. However, he lost my address and I didn't hear from him. But as fate would have it, our paths did cross again: we recognized each other one day at busy Waterloo Station in London!

We dated after that and Lloyd gave me a ring and asked me to marry him. Then he requested that his return home be deferred, and this was granted. Subsequently, he was posted to the Canadian Military Headquarters in London, and he managed to be billeted at our house in Wembley.

Six months after we first met we were married. I remember Lloyd and me filling out an application to get married, which he took back to his C.O. There was a three-months waiting period, a cooling off time. Then I had to have a blood test and a physical exam by a Canadian Army doctor. Once approval was granted, we went ahead with our wedding plans and had the banns read at St. John's Church for the required three Sundays in a row. Our wedding was on 23 February 1946, and we went to Brighton for our honeymoon. We both continued to work, and lived at my mother's house until we left England.

Lloyd returned to Canada in July 1946, and soon afterward I received word that I was to sail on 27 August from Southampton on the *Queen Mary*. I didn't have to stay over anywhere but went by train from London to Southampton and then directly to the ship, all in one day. My luggage, two big trunks and a large suitcase, was picked up at my home. I didn't have to apply for a passport to enter Canada. At that time, my marriage to a Canadian automatically made me a citizen.

We soon set sail for Canada, but the voyage across the Atlantic Ocean turned out to be very rough--bad enough for the storm to be written up in the papers when I arrived in Toronto. I remember having just one meal after we left Southampton and

> I soon decided to get a job but . . .
> I was told I "didn't sound Canadian."

then being very seasick. I shared a cabin with a Dutch war bride who spoke no English, and I felt very much alone. I expect she did too! We landed in Halifax, Nova Scotia, and from there I went by train to Toronto, arriving on Labor Day weekend. Lloyd was at the railway station to meet me, and we went to his parents' house in Toronto, where we lived for a time.

I soon decided to get a job but encountered some difficulty because I was told I had "no Canadian experience" or that I "didn't sound Canadian." I finally worked as a secretary for the Canadian Red Cross Society. We moved to our own home in Toronto in 1948, and in October our first son was born. Later we had two more sons and a daughter. Sadly, our little girl died while she was still a baby.

When Lloyd retired from his dental laboratory business in 1987, we sold our house in Toronto and moved to an apartment in Ottawa, not far from where two of our sons and their families lived. I have been a hospital volunteer for almost twenty years in Toronto and Ottawa and made many friendships over the years. Our three sons have given us seven fine grandchildren whom we enjoy.

For us, looking back after fifty years of marriage, fate played a wonderful role when we chanced to meet--twice.

CONGRESS PASSES BILL TO ADMIT FIANCÉES

An amendment to the Immigration Act, Public Law 471, allows alien fiancées and fiancés to enter the United States with the intention of being married to a U.S. citizen who is serving in, or who has been honorably discharged from, the U.S armed forces during World War II regardless of immigration quota limits.

New York Times, 25 June 1946

Representative Richard B. Russell of Georgia proposed the bill to allow foreign fiancées of GIs and fiancés of WACs and the like to be admitted to the U.S. for a three-month period in order for the engaged couples to marry. Individuals had to pay their own fare to come over and also were required to post a bond guaranteeing their return fare if the wedding failed to take place within the specified time.

Russell, a bachelor politician, said he did not know why GIs wanted to marry foreign girls, and he "deplored" it, especially since there were so many pretty American girls. Nevertheless, the "pressure from disgruntled veterans," who still wanted to wed their loved ones living overseas, had warranted the action. Congress approved the legislation, and on 28 June 1946, it was signed into law by President Truman.

Within the first twelve-month period, according to the Immigration and Naturalization Service, 3,349 aliens engaged to American citizens from countries around the globe entered the United States under this act.

For one couple, Joyce Curnow and Bob Hinze, it meant that their marriage would finally take place, three years after they first met and two years after their intended wedding date. It all started in 1943.

JOYCE:
I met Bob in October 1943 at a local dance in my hometown of Port Talbot, southern Wales. He was with the U.S. 109th Infantry Regiment, 28th Division, stationed in an old castle on the outskirts of town. The Yanks had a reputation of being very fast with the girls, but Bob won my folks over by bringing them rationed food like sugar and so on. He had already won my heart!

> ... his father wrote me a "no welcome" letter
> before he had even met me.

In February 1944 I was conscripted for war work by the government and sent to High Wycombe, Buckinghamshire to work in a factory making radar tubes for submarines. Bob came to see me there, and we became engaged. When Bob put in the papers for our marriage, however, his Commanding Officer held them up deliberately, knowing that the regiment would soon be in the invasion of Europe.

After D-Day, 6 June 1944, even though Bob was in the thick of the fighting, we wrote almost every day. Then in February 1945 I received a letter from him telling me to make arrangements for our wedding. The papers had finally come through, and he would be coming to Wales on leave in March. So I bought a white satin wedding dress in Cardiff and notified the minister of my church. All my relatives promised to donate the (rationed) ingredients for the wedding cake which my Gran made.

Two weeks before Bob was due to arrive I received a telegram saying he was wounded and in a hospital in France. You can imagine how I felt! But Bob was safe. It took Bob about three months to get back to his regiment; then in August 1945 they were sent back to the States. Bob would have been sent to the Pacific, but by that time the atom bomb had been dropped, Japan had surrendered and he had enough points to get out of the service. Thank the Lord.

Bob immediately sent me money to pay my fare over, but I couldn't come with the war brides as I was only a fiancée. Later, after applying for a visa I had to go to the American Embassy in London for one of those "stand-up naked" medicals before they would process my papers. I wonder if they ever found anything on any of the girls and, if they did, were they turned back? To make it worse, while I was still waiting to go to Bob, his father wrote me a "no welcome" letter before he had even met me.

At last, on 6 November 1946 I got passage on the *Queen Elizabeth* and docked in New York five days later. I took a train to Chicago where Bob and I were married in a church ceremony on 16 November 1946--me in my white satin wedding dress bought about two years before I got to wear it.

Bob's mother, a little lady of Norwegian background, made me welcome, but his father never made friends with me, although I did try very hard. It made a very tense atmosphere, especially since we lived with my in-laws for the first three years of our marriage. He always favored his other son's wife who was German like himself, and he deliberately praised her in my presence.

Nonetheless, over many years, we have had a good life together with a beautiful daughter, a fine son-in-law and two wonderful grandsons that we see a lot of. I felt honored, as a singer, to be called upon to sing the "Star-Spangled Banner" at Bob's annual regimental reunions. I am proud of my British heritage, but I am also proud that I have been an American citizen since May 1949.

The most exciting trip that we took back to Britain was in 1986 when we attended the first GI Brides Reunion that was held over there.

**26 September 1986: Joyce and Bob Hinze
at the 40th GI Brides Reunion, Southampton, England.**

Sitting on as World War II vintage jeep in front of the Guildhall.
Photograph by Sean Kelly

5

BACK TO BLIGHTY

First GI Brides Reunion "Over There"

September 1986, Southampton, England.

Coming home, that's what this reunion was about, this remarkable affirmation of the commitments they'd made as youngsters. They are grandmothers now, some are widows, and their husbands haven't worn khaki in decades.

Lynn Sherr, ABC TV, *20/20*

For the fortunate few, it was time to celebrate. The historic port-city of Southampton, through which two million GIs had passed and their 70,000 war brides had departed, hosted the GI Brides Reunion. It was the first official reunion of the GI brides to be held on British soil, and they came, many accompanied by their husbands, from twenty-six states. Other war brides came from Canada and Australia representing the British girls who had married servicemen from those countries during the war.

Most of the girls had been back to Britain to visit family and friends many times before this reunion was held. However, for one couple, Marguerite and Albert Couch of Walla Walla, Washington, it was their first visit back to Marguerite's homeland in forty years. For many, other priorities of life had dominated in the intervening years, but the 1980s and the 1990s seemed an opportune time for organized groups of people to reunite.

At the Southampton reunion, Terry Trucco, from the *New York Times*, made page one on 29 September 1986 with her report:

Warbrides go home to tea and tears.
It had all the makings of a first-rate 40 year reunion, with big band music, a lavish garden party, a special command performance by Dame Vera Lynn and tears . . . .

Dame Vera Lynn, center, talking in her dressing room in Southampton, England with Eunice Upchurch, left, and Vera Long, British women who married American soldiers in World War II.

29 September 1986

Jonathan Player, photographer.
Photo by permission of *The New York Times*

Southampton's large Grecian-like Guildhall was the hub for the Rendezvous Meeting Place, concerts and dances with The Glenn Miller Sounds played by Herb Miller (Glenn's brother) and the big band sound of Syd Lawrence, all honoring the delighted GI brides. But as people arrived for the opening "Welcome Party," they were startled at what confronted them. It was as if the clock had been whisked back to the military olive-drab and armored bustle of the Second World War.

Massed on the half-acre cobblestone forecourt of the Guildhall were vintage jeeps, staff-cars and tanks, all manned by GI uniformed servicemen who even sported regulation GI haircuts. These were young men who collected World War II memorabilia and re-enacted such wartime scenes as a hobby. Other men and women wearing a variety of Allied naval, air force and Red Cross uniforms added color and authenticity to the 1940 era charade.

Inside the Guildhall old friends met again, and new acquaintances were made. Sherry served in the ballroom was followed by a typical wartime meal that produced groans and chuckles from the crowd when "good ole" American spam appeared! More popular was the English-style fish and chips sprinkled with malt vinegar and served with "mushy" green peas.

Favorite songs of the 1940s filled the air. Singers from Southampton's musical society had dressed up in wartime uniforms, including practical one-piece siren-suits made popular by Winston Churchill, and turbans worn by factory girls to protect their hair from dangerous machinery. The evening's compère, Brian Godfrey, was authentically garbed as an Air Raid Warden--complete with "tin hat" and gas-mask hanging from his shoulder. Suddenly, the deafening wail of a resurrected air-raid siren surprised everybody and brought silence to the crowd in the ballroom, and shivers down the spine. For a little while, many an eye spilled with tears as memories of the war, and loved ones lost, came flooding back. Then all at once, the band struck up again playing familiar old British hits like the "Lambeth Walk," and a cheeky "Knees up Mother Brown!" It was time to step out to dance and sing, and then to get back into the American mood with more jitterbug and jive.

Scheduled for the next morning was a return visit to Tidworth and Bournemouth where the U.S. Army had processed the girls for their original trip to America after the end of World War II. A fleet of red and yellow double-decker tour buses drove up to take the group on this excursion. After a welcoming ceremony at Tidworth, and after a firm assurance from officials that there would be "No medicals today, girls!" a tour of the cold austere barracks followed. It was hard to imagine that this was the same place that, throughout most of 1946, had resounded with the voices of thousands of excited young war brides, some with noisy squirming babies, as they experienced several traumatic days of army-run immigration formalities.

Much less stark and more delightful was the next stop, at Bournemouth's ornate seaside Carlton Hotel where most of the girls with children had been housed. This time there were no food shortages, and instead an elegant afternoon tea, with cucumber and salmon sandwiches, pastries, strawberries and cream and all the trimmings, was daintily served by waitresses. Comfortably seated around small tables, it made a welcome respite on this journey into yesterday--to "summon up remembrance of things past."

Tragedy struck on this first full day of the reunion when sixty-year-old Mrs. Hilda Cye collapsed and died of a heart attack. She was a widow, living and working as a real estate agent in Florida, and had traveled to England alone. "Hilda was so excited to be here" said one of her friends quietly. "It was where she wanted to be."

The sun shone brightly for the following afternoon Garden Party at Broadlands House, the Palladian home of the esteemed war veteran and last Viceroy of India, the late Lord Louis Mountbatten. For the war brides, it was a day to wear flowered summer dresses and straw hats, to enjoy the landscaped gardens, the ornate fountain with goldfish darting around in the water, and to walk along the river that wound through the estate. Afternoon tea, laid out on tables inside a huge marquee, with music played by the Solent Brass Band, was the stuff the ladies had dreamed about when thinking of an ideal summer day in England. To make the day complete, Patience Strong, the much loved author and poet, read some of her wartime poems to the assembled group. An occasion to relish.

Those attending the reunion filled St. Mary's Church on Sunday for a service of Thanksgiving and remembrance. The church stands on the same site as one going back to the seventh-century, and it is the mother church of Southampton. It was damaged by German bombers several times in the 1940 blitz but had since been repaired, with its famous bells successfully mended and rehung. The well-known song "Bells of St.Mary's" dates from the First World War when the sound of St. Mary's bells echoing across the water near Southampton Docks inspired two soldiers to write it. During World War II Bing Crosby made the song his own in a popular American movie by the same name. But now, in ancient St. Mary's Church as the service of Thanksgiving continued, all hearts present were uplifted by the liturgy, and everyone sang the old familiar hymns with thankful gusto.

Ever present at the GI Brides Reunion were British, American and Canadian newspaper reporters and television crews who breezily competed with one another to cover this, the most sentimental of the World War II reunions. From the American Broadcasting Company in New York, producer Rob Wallace, senior editor Meredith White and correspondent Lynn Sherr were on hand with camera and sound crew to find a story behind the reunion. They did. It was shown in the States later, Thanksgiving Night 1986, on ABC's *20/20* (and repeated in 1992 on Christmas Night). Co-hosts, Barbara Walters and Hugh Downs introduced their sweeping historical documentary, "Falling for the Yanks," as the story of the "modern Pilgrim" British war brides going to America:

> Tonight, one of the most satisfying victories of World War II; how some 70,000 American GIs won the hearts of 70,000 British maidens. It's a never-before, never-again love story.

On the screen flashed 1942 period black-and-white wartime film clips from Pathé Gazette showing newsreels of troopships docking as the reporter's voice crisply informed the viewer that "more U.S. troops arrive in Britain." Then the Prime Minister, Winston Churchill, deftly put it all in a nutshell, as was his way:

> There was a time not long ago when for a whole year, we stood alone. Those days, thank God, are gone. We now move forward in a great and gallant company.

Over two million Yanks had arrived before D-Day, and, when most of them left for the June 1944 invasion that "would determine the fate of the free world," thousands of Anglo-American romances had already culminated in betrothals or marriages. The heart-warming accounts of several couples interviewed on the spot at the reunion by Lynn Sherr gave view to some wartime romances: Joyce, who sailed to Chicago after the war to marry her fiancé, Bob Hinze; Audrey Bradley, who had stayed on in

England to give birth to her son--and then received a telegram saying that her GI husband had divorced her; Alma Lackey, having been "extremely lonely" living in a snowy northern state, was elated when her husband suggested that they spend their retirement years in England; Vera and Charles Long, who "searched in vain for their honeymoon hotel" by the sea; and Jack Cherrington, who met Olive Cakebread at the Black Bear pub in Biggleswade, Bedforshire and announced to his buddies back at the

Olive Cakebread Cherrington
Served in the women's Land Army, 1942-1946.

barracks that night, "Boys, I just met the girl I'm going to marry!" A year later, on 27 October 1945, he did.

Lynn Sherr brought the *20/20* documentary of the GI Brides Reunion to a conclusion when, as their final event held in the Southampton Guildhall was shown, she said:

> Appropriately, the woman who had accompanied them throughout the war brought this reunion to a close, Dame Vera Lynn. Her music gave them hope ... and now it reminded them that their love had survived as well.

Wearing the Order of the British Empire on her white evening dress, Dame Vera Lynn, the wartime "Sweetheart of the Forces," sang the songs so familiar to her audience: favorites like "The White Cliffs of Dover," "When the Lights Go On Again" and "A Nightingale Sang in Berkeley Square." What was the great mystique about this singer? World-wide broadcasts of Vera Lynn's melodies throughout the war brought hope and inspiration to all who were separated from their loved ones. To those serving in the armed forces somewhere overseas and to those holding out on the home front, the sound of her voice was a vital link. "We'll Meet Again!" She achieved in music what Winston Churchill's patriotic words did in his stirring speeches--a bull's-eye for the English-speaking world and for all freedom loving people.

Dame Vera Lynn's audience in the Guildhall remembered, and the atmosphere seemed to tingle with emotion until the concert finished with a poignant finale, **"Now is the hour when we must say good-bye."**

Thus the reunion ended on a surge of bittersweet nostalgia, and the "brides" once again prepared to journey to the New World. This time they would travel by jet on a trip of only a few hours' duration. There was another difference. Now each one was returning to a familiar life and strong personal ties in America.

February 1946: Walter Clarkson & Paula Elizabeth Westerman
St. Marks Church, North Audley Street, London

1944: Walter first saw seventeen-year-old Paula when she was the dinner guest of a fellow officer at a Junior Officers Club in London. He discovered that she lived in Surbiton, a short bicycle ride (by crossing the Thames at Kingston) from his base in Bushy Park (SHAEF). Walter followed his heart--finding romance and love that would last forever.

WORLD WAR II VETERANS: 50 YEARS ON

"D-Day"

We will participate in the June 1994, D-Day, Fiftieth Anniversary ceremonies in Europe. In England, the high points will be commemorative events at Bushy Park, Middlesex; Grosvenor Square, London; a Memorial Service at Keble College Chapel, Oxford University for SHAEF members and our Allied colleagues, and a D-Day Garden Party at Southwick House, where General Eisenhower issued the order to launch the invasion. We will sail for France on the <u>Black Prince</u> *for the ceremonies on the Normandy beaches.*

Alan F. Reeves, Commander, *The SHAEF Communiqué,* March 1994.

Midway in the 1990s, numerous World War II groups like the SHAEF Veterans Association returned to wartime locales for Fiftieth anniversary reunions in keeping with historical commemorations as they befell. "Old soldiers never die," goes the well-known saying, but, before they "fade away," those who could go back would experience nostalgic journeys.

In 1985 the SHAEF Veterans Association was formed in the U.S. by Allen Petersen, who served as its first Commander. Many of those who had been assigned to either of Ike's two principal command headquarters, HQ/ETOUSA and then SHAEF, began to meet at annual reunions. And for special commemorative events in Europe, they join their British SHAEF associates.

Five decades earlier, *Overlord,* the Allied plan for storming Hitler's formidable defenses along the coast of Northern France, finally materialized. General Eisenhower was chosen Supreme Commander to lead the Allied Expeditionary Force on what he termed a "Crusade of Europe." Understandably, the D-Day* landings in Normandy on 6 June

---

***D-Day. D,** the first letter of Day + Day, was the unspecified date for the Normandy Invasion. The designation had been used during the First World War by the American Expeditionary Force for beginning its St. Mihiel offensive in France.

1944 and the VE-Day celebrations, nearly a year later, seem like "ancient history." But not to the survivors, with memories of their war still deeply etched in their hearts.

"Victory in Europe: VE-Day memories will highlight May 1995."

William C. Lahman, *The SHAEF Communiqué.*

A year after observing the milestone D-Day ceremonies, veteran commemorations during 1995 centered first on the end of the war in Europe with the defeat of Germany. On 8 May 1945, Hitler's "Thousand Year Reich" had fallen after twelve years of Nazi purges, slaughter and blitzkrieg invasions. A few months later, in August, the war in the Pacific ended when Japan surrendered. Thank God, the Allies had won the race against the Axis powers to produce the world's first atomic bomb. Peace on earth.

In May 1995 there was a great deal of attention again focused on western Europe as thousands of World War II veterans returned to the locales where they had served. American and British SHAEF veterans journeyed back to Versailles, Paris, Reims, Luxembourg and Frankfurt. For them, returning to the city of Reims was especially memorable. On 8 May, they visited the historic site of the German surrender, the "little red school house" where Colonel General Alfred Jodl, "acting by authority of the German High Command," had signed an unconditional "Act of Military Surrender" to the Supreme Commander, Allied Expeditionary Force; and simultaneously to the Supreme High Command of the Russian Red Army.

Afterward, the veterans attended an inter-faith memorial service at the Cathedral of Our Lady of Rheims. An original cantata "The War in the West," was performed, and readings of the wartime words of Winston Churchill, Charles de Gaulle and Franklin D. Roosevelt climaxed the service.

That same day in London, official VE-Day celebrations began symbolically with the sound of joyful church bells ringing. Under sunny skies in the city's great metropolitan open-air preserve, Hyde Park, a Peace Pageant was celebrated. And at Buckingham Palace, the Queen "Mum" Elizabeth, with her two daughters, Queen Elizabeth II and

Princess Margaret, stood on the high palace balcony and waved to huge cheering crowds below, just as they had done fifty years earlier with the late King George VI and Winston Churchill. In the United States, President William J. Clinton had invited World War II veterans to a national commemoration of VE-Day at Fort Myer, Virginia. With "A grateful nation remembers" as the patriotic theme of the day, the parade ground, Summerall Field, became alive with stirring pageantry. Clinton later joined world leaders attending solemn military parades in Paris and Moscow. Berlin was the site of concerts and conciliatory services. St. Paul's Cathedral in London, and many others, re-echoed this theme with services of remembrance, healing and peace.

Many SHAEF/ETOUSA GIs had been billeted in the United Kingdom long enough to have found and captivated the hearts of British girls. When these veterans meet annually, so likewise do their war brides, who still have not learned to say "tomayto" instead of "tomahto."

Several of the British girls who married those GIs had served in His Majesty's Forces during the Second World War and their stories appeared earlier. Here are more vignettes with SHAEF connections, told by Elsie, Alva, Allen (Kathleen's widower), Audrey, Joan, Ruby, and a French SHAEF bride, Claire.

SHAEF War Bride Connections

1945: Wedding party at St. Peter's Church, London
Michael and Elsie Schummer

On 3 March 1945, Elsie Cayless from Maida Vale, London, married Michael Schummer, U.S. Army, from Cincinnati, Ohio. Elsie was the young widow of a Royal Air Force pilot. She lived in London, working as a beautician until she was called up for war work at Hadley Page, an aircraft factory in Cricklewood. After her marriage to Mike, Elsie worked for a year at a U.S. Army Quarter-master's store in London.

ELSIE:

At the beginning of the war I married a pilot in the Royal Air Force. We had only been married a year when, in September 1941, he was killed in action.

Over a year later I met Mike at a New Year's Eve party given by a friend, Katherine Burbage. I was twenty-five years old then and Mike a year older. We dated, and, since I was working nights at the aircraft factory, Mike would leave me there after a date. Mike had arrived in London in May 1942 and was attached to an advanced party at the U.S. Embassy that later became part of Eisenhower's SHAEF organization. After D-Day, Mike, SHAEF G-3, was stationed in Versailles, Reims and Frankfurt.

We had no trouble getting U.S. military approval for our marriage. My family and friends said it was a good thing for me to get married again, and it had been over two years since Mike and I first met. Mike arrived in London from Paris on a week's leave, and we were married on 3 March 1945 at St. Peter's Church, Eaton Square, London. My younger brother is now Headmaster of the school there, by the way. After our wedding, Mike and I were able to spend a few days' honeymoon on the Isle of Wight.

Two months later the war in Europe was ending. On 7 May 1945, Mike was part of the SHAEF team at the red brick school house in Reims (The École Professionelle et Technique de Garçons) where the signing of the peace treaty between Germany and the Allies took place. A picture of Mike in *Life* magazine, 21 May 1945, shows him placing final copies of the treaty papers on tables at the schoolhouse. VE-Day was a day to remember for all of us.

After Japan surrendered, Mike returned to the States and was discharged. In February 1946 I received my travel orders and was sent to Tidworth. I had the usual physical there, but I particularly remember the German prisoners-of-war stoking up the fires in the morning in our rooms while we were still trying to get dressed! We sailed on the *Queen Mary*. I volunteered to help the hairdressers on board until I became too seasick to continue. I was very happy to see New York.

We landed 1 March 1946, and Mike met me at the dock. We stayed in New York for a few days, and I was very impressed with all the food and clothes--and no ration coupons needed. We traveled to Cincinnati, Ohio, and for the next two years we lived

I walk two miles with our dog, Maggie Thatcher . . .

with Mike's parents before we were able to find a place of our own. I loved America from the beginning and got along very well with all my in-laws. They were German and spoke that language all the time, so I had to learn some. One lady said to me, "You have been here for a year and cannot speak German." She had been here for twenty years and still could not speak English!

Everyone was nice to me. I worked in a department store as a hairdresser from 1947-88 when they tore the place down. Well, that was one way to get rid of me. I couldn't work as a beautician until I went to school for a year to get my American license, even though I had worked pro-fessionally in England. But, it enabled me to meet people and to get used to the different customs. I became a citizen in 1950. Sorry to say, we had no children.

The one thing I did have difficulty in was finding a church. Mike is Roman Catholic, and I had told him that I was not going to convert (we were married Church of England). The word, Episcopalian, didn't mean anything to me until I found out that it was an Anglican service. That meant a lot to me, and I have been very active in St. James' Church in Cincinnati for some time.

We built our house in 1955, just outside of Cincinnati, and we have a nice garden. I love to grow vegetables and flowers. The one thing that I miss is the sea, and I always desired to have a place overlooking the ocean. We have taken lots of vacations along the East Coast and Florida, and it's lovely to be near the sea.

I walk two miles with our dog, Maggie Thatcher, almost every day. I used to belong to a British Brides club, but it became too difficult to get to the meetings at night. My closest English friend died of cancer, and I really miss her. Years ago she was one of the first persons I met at the club, and our husbands got along too.

I was in the church choir and played the chimes, but my activities were curtailed when Mike became ill. Mike retired as an office supervisor for the Cincinnati Gas and Electric Company. He became ill with diabetes, Parkinson's disease, and had several strokes. He died in 1995, not long after our golden wedding anniversary.

Life has changed and I miss Mike. One thing that doesn't change though is my enjoyment of drinking a nice hot cup of tea, regardless of the weather. And I still use a tea-cozy to keep the teapot hot.

**Alva Bromley, twenty-two years old,
from Dobcross, near Oldham, Lancashire**

September 1939: Alva was attending Avery Hill College in Eltham, London, when war broke out. Later, from 1941-1945 she was an elementary school teacher (a wartime reserved occupation) in Stockport, Cheshire. She volunteered to be an air raid firewatcher.

ALVA:

The local Anglican church in Stockport, where I lived and was teaching, ran a canteen to welcome the Yanks who had been billeted temporarily in our suburb. I was there on duty one evening in February 1944 when Alan Reeves, U.S. Army, SHAEF, from Cleveland, Ohio turned up. We discovered we both liked music, and he took me to the Halle Orchestra concert the following Sunday afternoon. Things developed from there and we fell in love. Seventeen months later we were able to get married.

Alan arrived in England from Germany for our wedding, 26 July 1945, with my family and friends there to wish us happiness. Afterward we left for Swindon, Wiltshire, where Alan had been assigned to teach French at the American University at Shrivenham. A few months later Alan left for the U.S.A. to be officially discharged from the army. However, in January 1946, he returned to England to pursue his degree at Oxford University. Quite a few other American students were there, and I found them warm and friendly. Our first son, Christopher, was born in July while we were at Oxford. The following year, in August 1947, the three of us sailed together to our new life in America.

I was not a GI bride in the fullest sense of the word since I did not sail with them. Alan and I paid our own way to the States, traveling on the *Veendam*. I had obtained all necessary documents at the American Embassy in London. The only thing that struck me as odd was my encounter with U.S. immigration officials. I was in the early stages of pregnancy with David, holding thirteen-month Christopher on my lap, not feeling well in the tremendous summer heat at Hoboken, New Jersey, and the only thing they were interested in was whether I planned to overthrow the U.S. government by subversive means.

My first impression of America was the enormous amount of food available. I had a steak in New York the first night of my arrival, and it was the equivalent of one month's meat ration in England. On the train to Cleveland, Ohio, where Alan's family lived, I was shocked when the conductor called my young son a "cute little bugger." Everyone talked loudly and told me their first names. The buildings were bigger; the cars were bigger. Alan's family were very kind and supportive. I can't remember any discrimination from anyone. If anything, my British accent was an

| I claim two spiritual homes--London and San Francisco . . . |

asset, rather than a liability. After a visit of two weeks in Cleveland, we traveled by train to San Francisco where we made our first home.

In my early years in America, I was very British. I read my favorite children's books, like *Wind in the Willows, Alice in Wonderland* and the *William* books by Richmal Crompton, to my sons. I had loved them when young, and they loved them, too. I abandoned British meanings and spelling years ago after an hilarious experience when I told a group of people sitting around a fire that they looked extremely homely. In England, that's a "cozy" compliment!

In 1948 we returned to Cleveland for employment reasons and lived in the Midwest for the next ten years. It wasn't easy at first. I missed the ancient buildings of England, especially the cathedrals, which lend perspective to one's life. I found the increased pace of life disturbing. Nobody walked anywhere-- everybody drove. But then, to get to the countryside, one had to drive miles, no slipping through a gate into a farmer's field. It took me a long time to get used to houses without hedges or fences round their boundaries. One felt exposed. Things improved greatly for me when we moved to Washington, D.C. There I found history. Also elegant Georgian-type houses that reminded me of home. And the national news was local news, all very exciting.

San Francisco proved very fulfilling too, when we moved back there. By this time I had adapted myself to life in America. Geography was my major subject in college, so I was familiar with the topography and main industries of the U.S. I was also interested in the pioneers, particularly in New England and Virginia.

I became a U.S. citizen in 1951, and as an Anglo-American my double heritage brought me many blessings. I claim two spiritual homes--London and San Francisco, two cities of infinite variety and ineffable charm. My national heroes are Sir Thomas More and Thomas Jefferson, Sir Winston Churchill and Abraham Lincoln. The well-ordered English landscape and the magnificent American wilderness enhance my life with beauty.

I try to be diplomatic in talking about Britain to my friends. Americans are vulnerable in this area, and the overwhelming

... "our countrymen are all mankind."

affection I have about Britain might disconcert them. They generously indulge me, however, when I return from a British trip and start babbling about cathedrals, gardens, London streets and other delights of British life.

I've worked on and off over the years--taught in a private nursery school and worked as a children's librarian. In Washington D.C. I worked for the National Association of Broadcasters, and later, in San Francisco, I worked for the Federal government until I retired. Since then I've been a volunteer for the Red Cross, taken classes at the local university and written short stories. Alan and I travel a lot and are constantly drawn back to the U.K. and France. My first and foremost hobby is reading, especially British detective novels and Anglo-American classics.

One custom I shall never abandon is teatime around 4 p.m. It consists merely of tea and a cookie, but I make the tea properly in a teapot and serve it in good china. I find it not only a pleasant break in the day but oddly comforting. Now that Alan is Commander of the SHAEF Veterans Association, he stays busy organizing things. Our sons have families. Christopher is a management consultant and has two children, Joshua and Katy. David is a lawyer and has a young son, Michael. We love them madly and visit them often.

One of my greatest blessings has been the widening of my horizons: "My country, right or wrong" has given way to "our countrymen are all mankind."

Remembering Kathleen

On 19 December 1945, Kathleen Adkins Farrell from Twickenham, Middlesex married William Allen Hearne, U.S. Army, from Berkeley, California. Kathleen's narrative is by her husband, Allen. Sadly, Kathleen died in 1991 at the age of seventy-five in Ontario, California after suffering a heart attack.

1945: Cole Court Hotel, Twickenham, London

Kathleen and Allen Hearne

ALLEN:
    I know that Kathleen would have loved to participate, so I will try to do it for her. After all, we were married over forty-five years.
    Before I met Kathleen, she was married to a Royal Air Force pilot, Dennis Farrell. In 1941 he was killed in action, just two

> . . . she could eat one meal at the mess hall
> and no ration book coupons were needed!

months before their daughter Rosemary was born. This was a hard time for Kathleen. She had to give up her home, find a job and someone to take care of the baby and live with friends or relatives under crowded wartime conditions. While living in Teddington she was employed by the U.S. 8th Air Force in supply headquarters at Bushy Park. This job was ideal because she could eat one meal at the mess hall and no ration book coupons were needed!

I was assigned to SHAEF Headquarters Command in Bushy Park for a year, but I never met Kathleen until after I was sent to France. On my first leave I flew back to England to visit some of my old friends and arranged to meet them at the *Royal Oak* in Teddington. Kathleen was with the group. We agreed to meet the next day as I was a "poor lonesome soldier far from home." One week later, after having met her little girl and her parents, I proposed to Kathleen in the blackout on the platform of Kingston station. I told her that I wanted to take Rosemary (a lovely little girl of three years) back to the States some day, and I wanted her to come too--sort of a package deal. While she was catching her breath, my train came, and I went to Bovington Airport and flew back to Versailles, France.

As a junior officer I was sometimes sent on courier duty from France, Luxembourg or Germany back to London, so Kathleen and I kept in close touch. Finally, after VE-Day, having visited my chaplain and getting my CO's approval to marry, and, after having Kathleen sign papers that she loved me, wouldn't hold the U.S. responsible for anything or expect to have PX privileges and so on--although they might provide transportation to the United States if and when space was available--we were ready to get married with the U.S. Army's blessing.

We were married 19 December 1945 at St. Margaret's Church, Teddington. Wally Clarkson, who flew over with me from Frankfurt, served as my best man, and Kathleen's twin sister, Joan, was her attendant. We had a reception at the Cole Court Hotel in Twickenham and went to Bournemouth for our honeymoon. We came back to spend Christmas with little Rosemary and her grandparents, and a few days later my leave ended.

> The *Holbrook* always came to mind
> when tough situations arose during the rest of her life.

Before I left London, Kathleen and I went to the American Embassy, but it was closed. There was a sign that said "GI Brides Queuing Here." After that I had to leave Kathleen to make her own arrangements to leave England, to pack her treasures, get Rosemary ready, cope with officials at the U.S. State Department, the Immigration Services of two countries, follow Army procedures in a strange staging area, cross the Atlantic on a Brides Ship and get from New York to the West Coast on a troop train.

Kathleen sailed from Southampton on the *Holbrook* after going to Tidworth for processing and having a physical that she viewed with dismay. She had a miserable voyage, with Rosemary sick all the way, rough seas and frightening lifeboat drills. They were in a crowded cabin with other mothers and babies that cried all night.

They arrived in New York on 1 June 1946 but were kept on the ship for two days while awaiting an "O.K." from me in California! The *Holbrook* always came to mind when tough situations arose during the rest of her life. Finally, on the train to Berkeley, California, things got better. She cheered up when she was able to get some nylons in Chicago during the change of trains. Then we had a happy reunion in Berkeley.

Our first year together was not too easy. I had been a teacher before the war and went to work right away, but our biggest problem was housing. We lived in Richmond, California where many wartime Liberty Ships had been built. As the block apartments used by shipyard workers were vacated, the government reserved them for returning veterans with families. They were crowded, with minimal space, no sound proofing in the walls, no garages or storage space.

What a difference from the homes Kathleen knew in the Thames Valley! Our next-door neighbor, a former worker in the shipyard, seemed unusual to Kathleen because she had an anchor tattooed on one arm and a heart saying "Mother" on the other. This was something she had not counted on.

That is the way we got started, and things moved on well. We bought a home under a GI loan, our lovely daughter Carol was born in 1947, we planted a garden, went for more schooling under

> I know my bride was a good influence
> in our community as well as on me.

the GI Bill, and did all the things that thousands of other ex-GIs were doing. The area grew and prospered, the kids did well in school, and Kathleen became active in PTA, serving as president and on into high school through all the chairs.

Kathleen became a citizen after two years and then became active in civic affairs, the local Red Cross, the YMCA, Camp Fire Girls and the vestry of the local Episcopal Church. For years she belonged to the "Daughters of St. George" where she met other British war brides. I was always amazed at Kathleen's ability to tell what part of England someone was from if she happened to hear an English accent. She always said hello and asked if they were from the "West Country" or "East Anglia" and so on. To my ear they all sounded English, but sometimes they were Australians!

Today there is considerable concern about the excessive immigration to the United States, but I never heard concerns about the thousands of girls who came to this country from all over the world after the war. I think that they have been a good influence. I know my bride was a good influence in our community as well as on me. Before I was married, I had never been in an Anglican (Episcopal) church. I was a "Nothing" and had not been inside a church--except for funerals. Kathleen insisted that the girls attend Sunday School, and the church continues to influence all of our lives.

Our girls are married, and we have four grandsons and one great-granddaughter. In 1985 we celebrated our 40th wedding anniversary in our church social hall. And there, in 1991, the girls and I plus 200 friends attended Kathleen's memorial service. Our daughter Carol and her husband, who were both teaching in Kuala Lumpur, Malaysia, came to the memorial service, and Carol spoke. She ended by saying that she was comforted by something a Hindu told her before she left. "To my people your mother's death is a very good one. You come into this world as a tourist, see the sights, meet the people--then you go back to your home town."

Perhaps Kathleen would have wanted to see her life that way. She loved to travel, met many wonderful people. Now she's gone back home.

June 1946, John and Audrey Peters

**Audrey's wedding dress was sent to her
by John's family in America**

During the war, Audrey Jiggins lived with her family in Richmond, Surrey, on the outskirts of London, and worked for the Inland Revenue in Kingston. After the war was over, she married John and spent an exciting year with him in Berlin before going to the States. Living in Brooklyn was different and something of a challenge.

AUDREY:

I met John Peters, U.S. Army, SHAEF G-2, from Brooklyn, New York in June 1944 at the Richmond Ice Rink when I was sixteen and John was eighteen years old. I went with several girl friends, and John went with a group of buddies from SHAEF. When I fell on the ice, a smiling GI picked me up--John. Later, he loved to tell people that we first met when he "picked me up!" We met a few times after that. When he was transferred from Bushy Park, London to Paris, we wrote to each other. Every three months John returned on leave to see me, and he had some awful experiences trying to cross the English Channel. Once, he was held up at Calais for five miserable days because of the fog. One time ice caused his plane to skid off the runway, and another time the plane turned back because of engine trouble. Amazing what love will go through, isn't it? On the fourth leave John asked me to marry him.

We made plans for our wedding, and I was interviewed by a U.S. Army chaplain before the military approved our marriage. My family also approved, but John's parents were very much against our marriage. They felt that John was too young, also he hadn't finished his education and we had different religions. However, after our engagement they were very supportive and sent me my beautiful wedding gown, trousseau and many things then unavailable in wartime England.

We were married 1 June 1946 in Richmond, two years after we had met. After a honeymoon on the Isle of Wight, John returned to Germany. He was discharged from the Army and then worked for the U.S. War Department in Berlin, and that's where I joined him. Living there right after the war was very eventful and scary at times. I will never forget it. While we lived at the Officers Compound I made friends with a girl from Brighton, Winifred Marcott, who had married a GI from Brooklyn, John's home town, and we've remained friends ever since.

John and I left Berlin in October 1947 and traveled together to the U.S. We sailed from Bremerhaven on a hospital ship, the *Blanche Sigman* and were bunked separately in huge wards. I was near deck level, but John was near the bottom! It was a terrible stormy crossing, and the voyage took fifteen days instead of ten. There were a few English brides on board, but most were German, French and other nationalities. There were also American WACs returning home. I remember walking into the shower room the

> I asked her if she was talking about escalators--
> and she looked at me in shock!

first day and finding groups of German war brides talking together, completely naked and looking about eight-months pregnant. I had never seen anything like it before. We reached Staten Island, New York on l November 1947.

At first, we lived with John's parents in Bay Ridge, Brooklyn. Everyone was very friendly, and I remember neighbors bringing in their special dishes. John's family was from Ireland, Sweden and England, so their customs were not too different from mine. Apart from being homesick, I missed Sunday dinners and afternoon teas. The terrible heat in summer and the bitter cold in winter was different. I had a hard time pronouncing many names and getting used to ethnic foods. Now I find them delicious.

Living in New York City was exciting and really an education. I worked as a secretary in Manhattan and found the New York city subway noisy, rattling and scary, a big disappointment after London's underground system. Also the speed in which everything traveled, even the people, whom I thought extremely impolite as far as opening doors and so on.

Soon after we arrived in 1947, John's mother took me shopping to see the biggest department store in the world (Macy's) where I would see "stairs that moved up and down." I asked her if she was talking about escalators--and she looked at me in shock! She was even more shocked when I told her there were department stores with escalators in England.

I remember how I missed my family and friends. I was one of those reluctant war brides that wanted to stay near home. We lived near the water in Bay Ridge, and while standing on a hill I would watch the *Queen Elizabeth* and *Mary* sail past on their way to England. So near and yet so far. But in 1951, I was on the *Elizabeth* going home for four months. By then we had two daughters, Susan born in January 1949 and Katherine in June 1951. I always dressed our daughters alike in British style clothes, until they protested when about eight years of age. I still keep the British traditions with Christmas crackers, cakes and mince pies. And I'm still a British subject.

We moved to New Jersey several years ago and live within twenty minutes of our two daughters and their families. One daughter adopted two baby girls, and we also have two other grandchildren, a boy and a girl. We love being with all of them. John enjoyed working as an architect in nearby Manhattan until his retirement. During the winter I raise seeds for the garden and later spend hours outside gardening. I help in the English TRACE program when people write to me asking help in finding their American GI fathers from World War II.

I find it extremely important to keep in touch with other GI brides through clubs and veteran groups like SHAEF. John has the History Chair with the SHAEF Veterans Association, and we attend all their reunions.

**London 1945: Joan Moore and Allen Petersen
were engaged for two years while Allen
returned home to study at Princeton.**

**Allen's army jacket shows the ETOUSA shoulder patch.
The SHAEF patch is on his right sleeve.**

During the war and until 1947, Joan Moore lived with her parents in Hounslow, Middlesex. She was employed at the Glyn Mills Bank in Osterly and London. When working in London, a favorite meeting spot for Joan and Allen Petersen was on the steps of St. Martin-in-the Fields.

JOAN:

Allen Petersen came from Brooklyn, New York and was in the U.S. Army stationed at SHAEF Headquarters, Bushy Park, Teddington, when I met him in September 1944. It was at a dance, and his army friend was with a girl I knew who introduced us. We never went out alone on a date but were always with a group of friends. Three weeks after we met, Allen was shipped to France, and he asked if he could write to me, but I never thought I would see him again. We did correspond though and got to know each other better. He proposed via the mail, and we got engaged.

In the summer of 1945, Allen returned to England on a two-week furlough to see me and to give me a diamond engagement ring. Then, because of illness in his family, Allen was repatriated. The war finished, and Allen entered Princeton University, as he had planned to do before his army service. It looked as though it would be a long engagement.

It was March 1947 before Allen returned to England again. As he was a civilian by then, it was not necessary to obtain U.S. military approval for our marriage. Allen's family and a member of mine had tried to discourage us, but we were married 7 April 1947 at St. Paul's Church in Hounslow. We spent our honeymoon in Paris, Switzerland and England. We lived with my parents for a few months, and then together we sailed on the *De Grasse* from Southampton to New York City. We landed in September 1947, three years after we had first met.

I did not know much about America, and I found the hardest thing to get used to was the money. I walked around with a bag full of change since I only used the bills--I just couldn't sort out quarters, dimes and nickels, but understood then why the GIs in England had grumbled about our British coins. Allen's family and friends were very friendly. All in all, I was lucky and liked my new life. In 1952, I became an American citizen. Missing my family was the big thing, and every letter I wrote home was spattered with tear-stains.

We moved to our own place in Princeton, and I worked at the University Book Store and the Princeton Bank while Allen continued his studies. After he graduated, we moved to Metuchen, New Jersey, and Allen went to work for Thomas Cook while I worked for the British Broadcasting Company (BBC) in New York City.

> In fact my brother, John, married Allen's sister, Dorothy,
> making another transatlantic marriage in the family.

We had three children: John Allen in 1949 (sadly, deceased)
and two daughters, Karen and Kristine born in 1953 and 1958
respectively. They know quite a bit about my British traditions
and family. I was delighted when, in 1954, my sister and brother
moved to America, and we have remained close. In fact, my
brother, John, married Allen's sister, Dorothy, making another
transatlantic marriage in the family.

I've now been married to the same ex-GI for nearly fifty years.
Our family continues to grow, and we have seven grandchildren. I
enjoy knitting, gardening and reading in my spare time. In recent
years I've been happy to meet other GI Brides at reunions of the
SHAEF/ETOUSA Veterans Association. Allen, who was Commander
for eight years, organized the association in January 1985 for
World War II veterans who served at General Eisenhower's Headquarters. One of our most exciting annual reunions was held in
Abilene, Kansas to commemorate the 100th anniversary of Ike's
birth.

Some British SHAEF veterans in London, whom Allen tracked
down and encouraged, organized their own veterans association.
Joint activities during these retirement years continue to cement
our Anglo-American ties.

A friend of SHAEF

Eveline Ruby Clark lived with her family in Charlemont, near West Bromwich, Staffordshire. In 1939, when almost sixteen-years-old Ruby qualified for college, but the war started and she went instead to Griptons Business School in West Bromwich. Later, she was employed in war work as a printer at Manifoldia and then worked in an office at Chance Brothers. Ruby volunteered for the Air Raid Precautions (ARP) service.

RUBY:
It was July 1944 when I met Leo Roy, U.S. Army, who came from Teddy, Kentucky. My dad invited six Americans from Pheasey Farm to our house for tea on Sunday. These were American soldiers who had been wounded in combat during the D-Day invasion of Normandy, and Leo was one of them.

Pheasey Farm was a rehabilitation center at Barr Beacon where American soldiers were based. My dad was a veteran of The First World War, and during The Second World War, at age sixty-two, he served in the Home Guard. He had a lot of compassion for the soldiers and appreciated the sacrifices they had made to help us.

Leo and I knew each other for a year before we were married. It took six months for us to get U.S. military approval for our marriage, and by then we had celebrated VE-Day. I was never interviewed by a U.S. chaplain, and neither of our families or friends tried to discourage the step we were taking. Leo was back in Germany, but he was given a week's leave for our wedding.

We were married July 14, 1945 at All Saints Church in West Bromwich. We went to Southampton for a few days honeymoon before Leo went back to Germany. For the next two years I continued to live in England, and our son, Roger, and daughter, Jacqueline, were both born there. With the war finished, Leo had been able to spend some time with us at my home in Charlemont, before he returned to America.

Leo's father, in the States, signed papers as my sponsor, and I applied for transportation and waited for my travel orders to arrive. My youngest baby had to be six months old before the U.S. Army would let us travel. Finally, we had orders to go directly to Southampton, so, no Tidworth and no physical. Nearly two years

1945: Ruby and Leo Roy
in Charlemont, Staffordshire, England

It was two years before Ruby was able to sail to America

after the end of the war, we left England and sailed aboard the *U.S. Marine Slasher.* It was a hectic voyage with two babies and no help from anyone. I shared a cabin with two other brides and their children, and we all became friends. We kept in touch for years until we all moved around and lost contact. We arrived in New York City on July 3rd, 1947, my twenty-third birthday. I'll never forget the date!

> They loved to listen to me talk and to watch
> the difference in how I treated the babies.

Leo was there to meet us, and he took us to the farming
country of Teddy, Kentucky where we were to make our new
home. Leo's family were all farmers. I did not know much about
America except what I was told, and my first impressions were
good. Leo's relatives and friends made us welcome. They were all
very curious about me being English.

I had an audience every day starting at about 8 o'clock in the
morning. They loved to listen to me talk and to watch the
difference in how I treated the babies. They thought it was
wonderful. The hardest thing to get used to was the food and
different meal times. I was embarrassed when I first saw lightning
bugs and thought they were tiny flashlights.

After I arrived in Kentucky, we stayed a year. Later, when we
had moved to Cincinnati, our daughter Donna was born, and five
years later our last baby, Jamie, was born in Hamilton. I always
talked to my four children about England, and I have kept up
some British traditions.

Now, all these years later I am a widow. I keep busy in my
church club, with my family and things like my grandsons' ball
games. So far, I have ten grandchildren, and I enjoy every one of
them. I travel a lot and it's fun to get together with other GI
brides that I have met at the SHAEF reunions. Recently I visited
my family in England. It's still so beautiful there.

SHAEF FRENCH BRIDE

By the end of 1948, when the 28 December 1945 *War Brides Act* expired, over 8,000 French war brides had entered the United States. In addition, many alien fiancées or fiancés of American GIs (from about forty countries) were being admitted under Public Law 471, 29 June 1946, the *Fiancées Act*.

In 1947, Claire Jeanine Laumonier from Ste. Genevieve des Bois (Essonne), France, the fiancée of Vernon Hill, U.S. Army, from Trenary, Michigan arrived to be married in the United States. Claire was one of 784* French fiancées to come that year.

During World War II Claire was employed as a bank teller until after the liberation of France. Then she worked at SHAEF Communications Center, rue la Perouse, Paris.

In an unusual twist, Claire's widowed mother, Suzanne Laumonier Cochrane, was also a war bride, having married a Canadian serviceman during the war. In 1947, Suzanne was in America with her husband, living in Washington state, expecting to be reunited with Claire and to meet Vernon Hill, their future son-in-law.

Claire working at the SHAEF Signal Center in Paris

* During a four-year period, 30 June 1946 to 30 June 1950, U.S. Immigration and Naturalization Service records show that 8,538 fiancées and fiancés from countries worldwide entered the U.S.A.

1946: Claire in Paris

CLAIRE:

   I met my future husband early in 1946 when we worked in Paris at the same SHAEF communications center. In the days of Lend-Lease, the U.S. had furnished munitions and other war equipment to the French military. As part of the "pay-back" the French provided skilled workers to the various military installations. In this instance I was paid by the French government in francs and sent to work as a teletype operator. This involved the reception of encoded messages, as well as the transmissions to

... "there are plenty of fine young Frenchmen here"

various installations on the Continent, the United Kingdom and the Pentagon in the U.S.A.

Vernon had landed with American forces at Utah Beach, Normandy, twenty days after D-Day, and later on he was assigned to the SHAEF signal center in Paris as a technician for the maintenance of communications equipment. We met, and, throughout the working shift, we would see one another. More and more he would come, on any pretext, to see how my teletype machine was functioning, until one day we went on a date.

My father had died in 1941, and a few years later my mother married a Canadian and moved to Yakima, Washington. I lived with my grandmother, and more than once she discouraged me from dating an American by reminding me that "there are plenty of fine young Frenchmen here." My uncle was more blunt than that in expressing his views.

After Vernon and I had known one another for eighteen months, we became formally engaged, and he gave me a ring. Vernon's mother was very much in disfavor of him marrying a "foreigner." His parents had emigrated from Northern Europe to America, so they were newcomers themselves.

Vernon and I went together to the U.S. Embassy in Paris to formally apply for me to travel as a fiancée to the United States on a nonquota visa. We were aware that a Congressional Act made this possible. Early in 1947, Vernon returned to the States, and I had to pay my own fare and arrange my own ocean transportation. I had to have a physical at the U.S. Embassy. The receptionist, doctors and nurses there were condescending, rude, inconsiderate and generally treated me like a second-class citizen and as undeserving to travel and to live in the States. At the time it was quite disturbing.

It took about four months from my initial application until I sailed on the *Marine Jumper* from LeHavre. Besides the regular civilian passengers traveling on the ship, there were many other GI fiancées and wives aboard who came from various countries, including Germany. We ate cafeteria style and slept dormitory style.

We arrived in New York City on 27 June 1947. Vernon was there at the pier waiting to meet me, but my first impression of

> One aspect was the notion (particularly from males)
> that French women were "easy". . .

America was the nasty manner of the porter who helped me as we were disembarking, saying "Lady, that was hard work!" He was expecting or demanding a bigger tip.

It took me a while to comprehend the long distances in America, especially traveling from the dock in New York to Michigan to meet Vernon's family, and then to Washington State where my mother and stepfather lived. In France, one day's drive would take us to the border and into adjoining foreign countries. I also had to adjust my thinking from the European metric system to the English system of weights and measures: kilograms to pounds, kilometers to miles.

Meeting Vernon's family was probably a disappointment. They were not in the best of circumstances, yet Vernon had never misrepresented himself or his means. In fact, I thought his family and friends were quite crude.

We went on to Yakima, where my mother and stepfather resided, and were married there on 6 September 1947. We spent our honeymoon on the Pacific coast. After living in Yakima for a while, we moved to Omaha, Nebraska where my husband attended a Technical College. There I landed my first job as a teller at the Federal Reserve Bank in Omaha, and I felt that by being accepted I had "proven myself." One aspect that hung over for years was the notion (particularly from males) that French women were "easy" and that I would "fall over" whether married or not.

My husband's work as an electronic specialist with the Federal Aviation Administration took us to Fairbanks, Alaska for seven years. Our daughter, Jeanine, was born in 1952, and a year later our son, Robert, was born. I became a U.S. citizen while in Fairbanks.

There were many new customs that I had to get used to in America, such as having meals served "family style" and having several items on the plate all at once. In France, the vegetables or "side dishes" were served in sequence, with the entree and the salad served last. One thing I could not accept immediately was being served coffee with the meal instead of later. Also, I was surprised that most houses had no gates or fences but were quite

> I had heard that Chicago had lots of
> gangsters (certainly not the place to go) . . . .

open. In France, stone or metal gates and fences generally surrounded a home.

Funerals were a definite surprise with bright colors being worn and with laughing and carrying on at the viewing, whereas in France, there seemed to be a lot of wailing and grief and black dresses for women and black suits for men.

We'd like to visit France one more time, but I am a fearful flyer which restricts our travels. This may be a long-delayed reaction to seeing air battles and planes being shot out of the sky. In one instance a German plane crashed near my house, and the pilot was completely incinerated.

I did not know much about America except that it was far away, that it was much larger than France, and that English was spoken. I had heard that Chicago had lots of gangsters (certainly not the place to go) and that the wild West was inhabited by Cowboys and Indians.

Being young, twenty years old, I think it was a lark or an adventure, yet I made a commitment to a lifelong relationship with my future husband, and we have been happily married ever since.

CHEERIO!

An Ode to the British War Brides

War Brides. What a bond between us
Blest be the bond that ties
Thousands of us crossed the ocean
Pilgrim mothers, Pilgrim wives
Crossed it with our tears and longings
Bridged the ocean with our love
Paved the way for better reasoning
Gave a nation its new blood
Oh! I'm proud to be a War Bride
Sharing all the battle scars
But how I miss my dear, dear England
And does She ever cry afar,
Is She well--and is She happy
Though come the very host of hell
I hear London calling. Big Ben speaking
Listen! All dear British Daughters
Nine o'clock--and ALL IS WELL!

Hazel Raeburn Garrison, war bride from Plymouth, Devon.

We came throughout 1946, the peak period for war brides from overseas to reach America, arriving by shiploads, not as political or religious asylum seekers or illegal immigrants seeking an easier way of life, but as legally wedded brides of U.S. soldier-grooms. We had patiently endured U.S. Army and governmental red tape, finger printing, the indignities of a flashlight body search, a check for lice, infections or some nasty disease unmentionable in that day's polite society, and when asked, swore we would not plot nor do harm to the U.S. Government. Marriage to a GI serviceman had not automatically given us U.S. citizenship, as it had to World War I foreign war brides. In 1922, this right was abolished with the passage of the *Cable Act*. Immigration laws in effect during the 1940s were very restrictive, and a quota system enacted in 1924, the *Selective Immigration Act*, established the yearly number of people allowed to enter the States from each country. The annual number was not to exceed 150,000. We knew we were privileged in this respect because we were entering the country as nonquota aliens under a 1945 special act of congress. Still, as aliens, we had to be sponsored by "a citizen" with a pledge that as newcomers we would not become a financial burden to the United States. And, U.S. immigration officials had the power to deny entry to any immigrant because of health reasons or some other technicality.

Coming from the bosom of the Mother Country, we took our civil "rights" for granted, qualified only by the fact that we were women. We had plenty of rights compared to females living world-wide, but we still knew our place in a male dominated Western society. We were young, curious and eager to understand and tackle a fresh environment in a new land, to blend in and yet to mark it with our own stamp, to share our ideas and ways with our loved ones. So we arrived, sometimes hearing the loud cries of American girls shouting, "Go back home!" Had we really pinched someone's boyfriend? All's fair in love and war, it's said. It brought to mind Christmas 1936, after the abdication of King Edward VIII in order to marry Wallis Simpson, the elegant American divorcée. When carol singing as youngsters that year, we had cheekily sung in full voice, "Mrs. Simpson's pinched our King" to the tune of "Hark! the Herald Angels Sing." Now, ten years later, the shoe was on the other foot! It was still all for love.

Historically, the 1946 mass sailing of thousands of GI Pilgrim Brides to the New World had signaled the ending of a great American migration era, when crossing an ocean had been possible only by boat. For Europeans, the port of New York had long played a profound role in the lives of incoming boatloads of settlers, and for nearly a century the first stop for millions had been the dreaded Immigration Center on Ellis Island. But following World War II, this near-empty facility would close down as a point of entry into the United States and eventually become a popular historical immigration landmark when it reopened to tourists and roots-seeking citizens.

The dramatic shift from passenger ships to jet planes that was gradually taking place would make travel that much faster for people, the world that much smaller. When this happened, the last major "American frontier" had been overcome. Until then, crossing the seemingly endless ocean had remained a daunting hurdle that each wave of European settlers faced, even long after America's mainland and "Western frontiers" had been conquered. Future immigrants, however, would still face the personal trauma of homesickness and loneliness as they settled in a new land.

It is fitting to recall the words spoken in January 1946 by U.S. Transport Commander, Colonel Floyd Lyle, as he greeted the first eager group of young British GI brides on board the *Argentina*:

> Welcome to the United States, for even now on the decks of an American liner you are on American soil. We are cousins, not of blood and language alone, but in a heritage of freedom and democracy which goes back to the Magna Carta. May you find warm hearts and kindness, peace and happiness even in a far country.

I sailed on the *Queen Mary* on her 30 March 1946 voyage to New York, one of 3,000 GI dependents aboard. There were a few first-class passengers including Lord Woolton, who, as Minister of Food during the war with its acute shortages and belt-tightening food rationing, was very well-known to the British public. Sailing with the war brides, he told us:

> You are a grand missionary army, bringing understanding between two countries. If you do your job properly, you will help to make the Americans understand the British. And I hope you will tell your people at home all that is good about America. I wish you good luck, happiness in your homes and prosperity in your work.

Throughout the war, Lord Woolton had been on the receiving end of much advice from the Prime Minister, Winston Churchill, about the allocation of food supplies to the public in their wartime island fortress, and on 14 June 1941, Churchill wrote:

> Have you done justice to **rabbit production**? Although rabbits are not by themselves nourishing, they are a good mitigation of vegetarianism. They eat mainly grass and greenstuffs, so what is the harm in encouraging their multiplication in captivity?

An illustration of how desirable rabbits had become to a hungry public is shown in a March 1944 letter written by the Earl of Warwick, while on

naval leave visiting his country estate, Warwick Castle, and sent to his
secretary, Hilda Cracknell Prouse, in London:

My dear Prowsie,

Eight rabbits will arrive on Friday. Three for Lady Throckmorton, two
for Mrs. Lutyens, one for the flat (tell Mildred), two for Dr. Harvey. And
ring the various people to arrange for delivery. Weather lovely but cold.
W.

Rabbits aside, Churchill viewed with alarm any "massacre of sheep
and oxen. The reserve on the hoof is our main standby," he declared. For
his part, Lord Woolton went on to educate the public about fortifying their
meager food rations by eating more homegrown vegetables. He skillfully
used Dr. Carrot and Potato Pete advertisements, *Kitchen Front* radio
chats and *Food Flashes* on cinema screens to do the job. In May 1941, the
head chef at London's Savoy Hotel introduced the "Woolton Pie" made of
vegetables, oatmeal stock, potato crust and gravy. It produced "hollow
laughs" for the rest of the war.

Fortunately for the British people, America and Canada in the West
and Australia and New Zealand "down under" helped greatly with
supplies of powdered eggs, tinned Spam, American style bacon, wheat
and many other precious goods that managed to cross the oceans safely
until peace had been won.

Enduring the bloodshed, bitterness and horror that was World War II,
the human spirit survived, and for the most fortunate ones it triumphed in
new found and lasting love. The GI pilgrim brides and their grooms were
among those who bore witness to this. Except for wartime and early postwar news about the "brides," the only publicity later was the "I told you
so" horror tales of hardships, betrayal and divorce. Of course, stories
about ordinary and successful relationships of any kind are not as
newsworthy, nor are they what authors give much space to. David
Reynolds, in his 1995 book about the WWII American "occupation" of
Britain, explores the fortunes of wartime marriages in a chapter headed
"Happily Ever After?" with a question mark, making happiness for
these couples appear extrememly doubtful. Like the old song that
"accentuates the positive," this retrospect pays special tribute to the vast
majority who have "made it," whilst it salutes all the war brides and grooms.

As time passes, the misty saga of the World War II foreign born GI brides will be further explored. North America has benefited from the diverse cultures of many races, starting with the migrating tribes that arrived here in prehistoric times, then in more recent centuries, by waves of various European explorers and settlers, Africans, Asians, Hispanics and others.

The British war brides, who shared an ethnic kinship with the Pilgrims of early Colonial American history have done much to enhance the use of the English language and to reinforce the spirit of fair play, liberty with order and justice for all. Those tenets, which they were reared under, stem mainly from the 1215 Great Charter of King John, the Habeas Corpus Act of 1679 and the English Bill of Rights of 1689. "We are born free" declared John Locke in 1681 and have "inalienable rights to life, liberty and estate." Those and other significant historical measures that at first benefited only white males of wealth and property led with increasingly giant steps to democratic freedom and responsibility for all citizens. The ascent of the "Common Man" is reflected in Great Britain's unwritten Constitution, common law, jury system, constitutional debate, and after the 1776 rebellion when the colonies fought to preserve (not obtain) such liberty, it inevitably resulted in the milestone United States Constitution and the Bill of Rights. These newcomers from Great Britain had ancient bonds and ties aplenty with America.

In teasingly good spirit, some of the girls were greeted by remarks like "Welcome to the Colonies!" when they arrived. "You're one of us now, so forget the Old Country." Paradoxically, after the political Revolution, United States history had cast King George III and his people as dastardly "villains" while the Founding Fathers, themselves British nationals, who benefited from the established colonial infrastructure, appear with nary a blemish nor wart. Over two centuries ago, perhaps a new nation had to burst forth to independence that way, but times and perspectives change. Possessing a good sense of humor and bits of homespun British witticism usually helped the girls, especially when any identity crisis unexpectedly loomed.

Not surprisingly, when they arrived, the girls found that the English language had indeed been Americanized, and many words were pronounced and spelled differently. The "u" was left out in colour, labour and neighbour; one "l" had disappeared from travelled and woollen; plough now became plow, a cheque a check, a car tyre a tire and the "h" in herb silent in America. Then the girls learned not to call anyone "a silly ass!" which was quite acceptable in England, and it was considered shocking in America to tell a downhearted man to "keep your pecker up" when they simply meant "chin up!" of course.

In 1986, a GI Bride Project was established at the Imperial War Museum in London for a collection of oral histories and records, under the leadership of Dr. Jan Stovold. Then in 1987, the Arthur and Elizabeth Schlesinger Library on the History of Women in America (at Radcliffe College in Massachusetts) added to its archives a collection of documents, photographs and research papers about the overseas war brides. These were important steps in making "something we don't read about in American history books" more readily available for future generations.

Marriages born in war. They sailed to America and 'twas "all for the love of you," an *American Dream* tied up in a wedding knot that carried the hearts of war brides to join their waiting husbands. **This** aspect of the war is easily dismissed as trifling, yet it signifies what life is all about: that it is worth fighting to have such freedom of choice in finding love and personal happiness.

Since these ladies arrived over fifty years ago in "the summer of their youth" (Edward Moore), they have touched the lives of countless Americans. In a reflective mood, the British war brides perceive how their lives were ultimately enriched by bridging two worlds--two countries, the land of their birth and the land they had wed. They cherish both countries as their own, and proudly reaffirm the common heritage of a four-centuries-old cultural relationship.

*   *   *   *   *

EPILOGUE

A War Baby Remembers

In the background of every memory is Mom's English accent and her expressions:

Night, night. Sleep tight.
Don't let the bugs bite.
If they do, you tell me.
I'll make a cup of tea.

I was born on 20 July 1945 to a war bride, Agnes Hayden Brooks, in the front parlor of my grandmother's house in Manchester, England. My father, Phillip Brooks, U.S. Army, was in England at the time.

My grandfather died suddenly in January 1946, delaying our scheduled departure to America. Mom sent a telegram to dad informing him of the change of plans. It arrived too late. Dad drove to New York only to discover that we were not on the ship. He drove back to Washington D.C. quite distraught until he found the telegram. It was a tumultuous time for everyone.

A month later, when I was seven months old, Mom and I arrived in New York aboard the *Santa Paula*. I wore a white fake fur coat, a parting gift from my grandmother. Mom said that I looked lovely wearing it.

Dad took us to our new home, a temporary housing unit, called Pickett Homes, in Arlington, Virginia. We arrived in the dark on a cold night to an empty place. The people next door came over and invited us to spend the night with them. Dad would have accepted this invitation from strangers but Mom was too shy. We slept on the floor that night.

We lived there for eight years. It was a tiny place built during the war with cement floors, cinder block walls, a coal stove and no bathtub. Dad worked full time for the government, went to college at night on the GI Bill, and drove a taxi on evenings and weekends. Mom did everything possible to become Americanized.

Christine Brooks, four years old

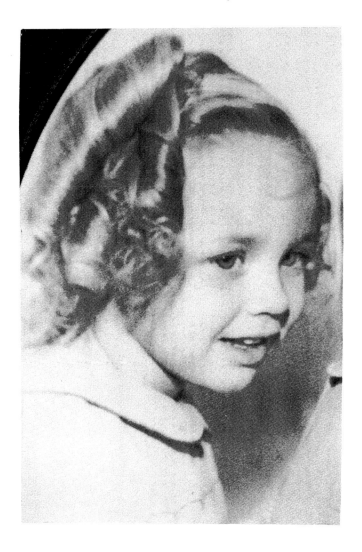

As a young child I was aware that Mom was struggling, literally and figuratively. I saw that she found many things confusing and others frightening. She blustered her way through ridicule by saying, "This is the way we did it in England." But she was not just struggling to learn American ways. More than anything she was struggling with unbearable grief: the loss of her world. Back in England she had been surrounded by her large family and during the war she was a supervisor in a factory. She had been confident and competent. All that was gone.

I saw that letters from England were savored and her treasure. She held me on her lap as she pored over them. She kept them folded in her large black purse and re-read them often. Severe homesickness engulfed her. Somehow, as a baby and toddler I felt her pain. I was Mom's sustaining beacon of hope through these difficult early years. I was her confidante for a lifetime.

Dad worked for the State Department. During the years 1956-1959 our family lived in New Delhi, India. While there, Mom became friends with English, Australian and Indian women as well as other Americans. In this international setting I discovered that we had a rich heritage, and for the first time I felt proud of Mom's English background, and mine.

Mom and dad had five children but I am the only one who was born in England. I am the only one who has gone back and visited our relatives over there. Now, I have a fantasy about retiring in England one day.

Christine Brooks Hopson
1997

December 28, 1945: *THE WAR BRIDES ACT*

[CHAPTER 591]

AN ACT

To expedite the admission to the United States of alien spouses and alien minor children of citizen members of the United States armed forces.

December 28, 1945
[H. R. 4857]

[Public Law 271]

Be it enacted by the Senate and House of Representatives of the United States of America in Congress assembled, That notwithstanding any of the several clauses of section 3 of the Act of February 5, 1917, excluding physically and mentally defective aliens, and notwithstanding the documentary requirements of any of the immigration laws or regulations, Executive orders, or Presidential proclamations issued thereunder, alien spouses or alien children of United States citizens serving in, or having an honorable discharge certificate from the armed forces of the United States during the Second World War shall, if otherwise admissible under the immigration laws and if application for admission is made within three years of the effective date of this Act, be admitted to the United States: *Provided,* That every alien of the foregoing description shall be medically examined at the time of arrival in accordance with the provisions of section 16 of the Act of February 5, 1917, and if found suffering from any disability which would be the basis for a ground of exclusion except for the provision of this Act, the Immigration and Naturalization Service shall forthwith notify the appropriate public medical officer of the local community to which the alien is destined: *Provided further,* That the provisions of this Act shall not affect the duties of the United States Public Health Service so far as they relate to quarantinable diseases.

Admission of certain aliens.
39 Stat. 875.
8 U. S. C. § 136;
Supp. IV, § 136.

Medical examination on arrival.
39 Stat. 885.
8 U. S. C., Supp. IV, § 152.

Quarantinable diseases.

Sec. 2. Regardless of section 9 of the Immigration Act of 1924, any alien admitted under section 1 of this Act shall be deemed to be a nonquota immigrant as defined in section 4 (a) of the Immigration Act of 1924.

43 Stat. 157.
8 U. S. C. § 209.

43 Stat. 155.
8 U. S. C. § 204.

Sec. 3. Any alien admitted under section 1 of this Act who at any time returns to the United States after a temporary absence abroad shall not be excluded because of the disability or disabilities that existed at the time of that admission.

Readmission after temporary absence abroad.

Sec. 4. No fine or penalty shall be imposed under the Act of February 5, 1917, except those arising under section 14, because of the transportation to the United States of any alien admitted under this Act.

Fines and penalties.
39 Stat. 884.
8 U. S. C. § 150.

Sec. 5. For the purpose of this Act, the Second World War shall be deemed to have commenced on December 7, 1941, and to have ceased upon the termination of hostilities as declared by the President or by a joint resolution of Congress.

Approved December 28, 1945.

Appendix B

U. S. Army War History, HQ European Command
Table III
War Bride Dependents Shipped from the European Theater, 8 May 1945 to 30 June 1946

DATE SAILED	U. K. BASE SOUTHAMPTON				WESTERN BASE LEHAVRE				BREMERHAVEN		
	SHIP	ADULTS	INFANTS	TOTAL	SHIP	ADULTS	INFANTS	TOTAL	ADULTS	INFANTS	TOTAL
Before March '46		6890	2649	9539							
4 March 1946	Santa Paula	285	91	376							
5 March					Goethals	434	16	450			
7 March	Gibbons	320	134	454							
8 March	Saturnia	550	207	757							
12 March					Vulcania	536	37	573			
13 March	Queen Mary	1588	746	2334							
14 March	Vulcania	292	38	330							
18 March	Alexander	953	265	1218							
19 March	Pres Tyler and Washington	1166	416	1582	Zebulon Vance	426	43	469			
20 March	Parker	150	51	201							
21 March	Ericsson	746	186	932							
22 March	Cristobal	152	57	209							
23 March	Bridgeport	370	107	477							
24 March					Brazil	395	46	441			
25 March	Uruguay	350	113	463							
29 March					Santa Paula	184	31	215			
30 March	Queen Mary and Holbrook	2336	782	3118							
4 April 1946											
6 April	Gibbons	311	135	446	Goethals	405	53	458			
12 April	Washington	723	284	1007							
16 April	Queen Mary	1635	699	2334							
17 April					Brazil	373	49	422			

DATE SAILED	U.K. BASE SOUTHAMPTON				WESTERN BASE LEHAVRE				BREMERHAVEN		
	SHIP	ADULTS	INFANTS	TOTAL	SHIP	ADULTS	INFANTS	TOTAL	ADULTS	INFANTS	TOTAL
19 April	Saturnia	973	267	1240							
20 April	Huddleston										
	Ericsson,										
	Cristobal	1162	302	1464	Santa Paula	289	43	332			
21 April											
22 April	Alexander	511	387	898							
27 April	Holbrook	622	164	786							
29 April	Parker	138	58	196							
1 May 1946											
4 May	Queen Mary	850	449	1299	Bridgeport	395	49	444			
7 May	Barry	397	127	524	Zebulon Vance	370	56	426			
9 May	Washington	640	259	899							
10 May	President Tyler	424	146	570							
11 May					Brazil	205	35	240	88	4	92
					Goethals	243	45	288	109	3	112
20 May	Ericsson	552	71	623							
22 May	Gibbons	240	159	399	Santa Paula	156	47	203	71	9	80
24 May	Saturnia	693	306	999							
26 May	Holbrook	557	209	766							
27 May					Cristobal	120	27	147			
6 June 1946					Brazil	226	49	275	39	4	43
17 June					Santa Paula	167	19	186			
19 June	Alexander	496	228	724							
20 June	Ericsson	396	63	459							
21 June	Bridgeport	279	120	399							
26 June	Goethals	246	76	322							
27 June	Zebulon Vance	266	89	355	Gibbons	186	16	202	89	23	112
					Brazil	190	12	202	130	20	150
8 May 1945 to 30 June 1946		TOTAL:		48,338			TOTAL:	5,983		TOTAL:	589

Participants

Sincere thanks to the following who gave me permission to use their names, stories and photographs for this book.

Amsbaugh, Doris Norley
Batten, Iris Barber
Braithwaite, Gilbert
Carter, Jean Holder
Cherrington, Olive Cakebread
Crocus, Dorothy Peers
Cubley, Joyce Howlett
Donellan, Ada Dimmock
Ferguson, Dorothy Sephton
Garman, Margaret Willis
Garrison, Hazel Raeburn
Grawey, Annette Bridges Langenberg
Harrington, Nancy West
Harris, June Marston
Hearne, William Allen
Hill, Claire Laumonier
Hinze, Joyce Curnow
Hopson, Christine Brooks
Karten, Eileen Wright
Kriegler, Doreen Timmins
Leon, Mary Boyle
Moran, Patricia Grimshaw
Peters, Audrey Jiggins
Petersen, Joan Moore
Quinn, Elizabeth Spirit
Racy, Eileen Fordham
Raven, Daphne Butcher
Reeves, Alva Bromley
Riley, Doris Dark
Roy, Ruby Clark
Schummer, Elsie Cayless
Scott, Daphne Fensom
Spencer, John
Stapp, Anne MacRae
Stern, Audrey Firkin
Taylor, Olive Howe
Upchurch, Eunice Isaac
Walker, Joan Atyeo

NOTES

Sources are listed in the order in which the subject appears, by section.

PROLOGUE   Pages xi-xiv

Stephen Brooks, *Bomber* (Imperial War Museum) 1983, 22. The air raid warning immediately after war was declared, 3 September 1939, was not caused by approaching Luftwaffe planes, but by the "ill-timed" flight of the French military attaché heading for London.

David Johnson, *V-1 V-2: Hitler's Vengeance on London* (New York, 1982), 194. On 27 March 1945 the final V-2 rockets (fired from Holland) fell on Stepney, East London and Orpington, Kent. Two days later, Hitler's last V-I pilotless planes attacked and exploded in the north of London.

INTRODUCTION   Pages xv-xix

William Shakespeare, "wondrous strange" *Hamlet*, I.v. 164; "journey's end" *Othello*, V. ii. 266.

Elizabeth Valentine, "The Girls They Didn't Leave Behind Them," *New York Times*, 10 February 1946, Sec. 6, 16.

U.S. Department of Justice, Immigration and Naturalization Service. INS 1949 typescript, RG 322: Under the *War Brides Act*, Public Law 271, 28 December 1945 to 31 December 1948, 117,683 aliens (112,882 women, 322 war grooms and 4,479 children) entered the U.S.A. NOTE: 25,877 babies of U.S. armed forces were admitted as U.S. citizens when accompanied by their "alien war bride" mothers. In addition, 10,826 persons "changed their status from non-immigrants to immigrants" under an amendment (Public Law 213, 22 July 1947) to the *War Brides Act*, to include "racially ineligible races."

"The Petticoat Pilgrims," *London Daily Express*, 11 February 1973, 5. Quotes reporter, Geoffrey Parkhouse.

John C. Miller, *The First Frontier: Life in Colonial America* (New York, 1966), 27. Convicts and "sturdy beggars," to serve as apprentices, had been sent to Virginia before the "maydens" arrived and the colony later "established."

Department of Justice, INS 1941 typescript, RG 322. Americanization classes before WWII. Many GIs (26%) had foreign born parents.

"Falling for the Yanks," produced by Rob Wallace, ABC News *20/20*, first shown Thanksgiving, 27 November 1986 and repeated Christmas, 25 December 1992. Quoting Lynn Sherr, correspondent, "not in American history books."

Lee Kennett, *G.I.: The American Soldier in World War II* (New York, 1987), 96, "parentheses."

PART ONE   1939-1945: Background in Great Britain   Pages 1-12

New York Times, 29 July 1945, 10, Hitler's invasion plans.

Richard Hough and Denis Richards, *The Battle of Britain: The Greatest Air Battle of World War II* (New York, 1989), 308, Royal Air Force.

Len Deighton and Max Hastings, *Battle of Britain* (London, 1990), 89. RAF leadership of Sir Hugh Dowding.

Winston Churchill, *The Second World War: Their Finest Hour*, Vol.II (New York, 1985), 297, invasion of England postponed; 322, Coventry Cathedral and the old city was "incinerated" in November 1940 air raids.

Johnson, *V-1 V-2: Hitler's Vengeance on London*, 190. Civilian's V-2 rocket description. 35,000 civilians were killed or seriously injured.

Winston Churchill, *The Second World War: The Grand Alliance*, Vol.III (Boston, 1985), 42, casualties; 3, quotation.

Norman Longmate, *The G.I.'s: The Americans in Britain 1942-1945* (New York, 1975), 10, "The arrival of the 34th U.S. Infantry Division in Belfast was a milestone in the history of Anglo-American relations and in the course of the Second World War." 2, Eamon DeValera's government in the Irish Republic stayed neutral throughout WWII.

David Reynolds, *Rich Relations: The American Occupation of Britain, 1942-1945* (New York, 1995), 118, "Irish neutrality." *A Pocket Guide to Northern Ireland* (Washington, D.C., 1942), 11, quotation.

David Hutchings, *RMS Queen Mary: 50 Years of Splendour* (Southampton, 1988), 35, "GI shuttle"; 37, the *Queen Mary* "did her bit" during WWII by carrying 810,730 Allied servicemen while sailing 661,771 miles around the world.

Bradley F. Smith, *The Ultra Magic Deals: And the Most Secret Special Relationship, 1940-1946* (Novato, CA, 1992), 151, BRUSA (British-American) agreement.

Thomas Parrish, *The Ultra Americans: The U.S. Role in Breaking the Nazi Codes* (Briarcliff Manor, New York, 1986), 120, "Bombe."

Charles W. Long, "As I Remember It," *SHAEF Communique* #34, 15 September 1995, 5-6. Publication of the SHAEF/ETOUSA Veterans Association. NOTE: Before 1943, GCHQ, Government Communications Headquarters, at Bletchley Park was known as GCCS, Government Codes and Ciphers School.

U.S. Army Air Force (during WWII). The Air Force separated from the Army in 1947 and became a new branch of the U.S. armed forces.

The Sunday Times, 5 June 1994, 1, Sir Bernard Montgomery's dedication to his troops. Also Churchill's quotation.

"Gee Honey, Your Hair Smells So Sweet!"   Pages 13-19

John Costello, *Virtue Under Fire* (Boston, 1985), 28, conscription of women.

Gwen Bradley Scruggs, quote "chewing gum" from ABC News *20/20*, Thanksgiving 1986.

Longmate, *The G.I.'s* (London, 1975), 104-5. In 1973 Summersby denied reports that General Marshall dissuaded "Ike" from divorcing his wife to marry her. Summersby acknowledged that she "greatly admired Ike" but she died in 1975 "with the full facts unrevealed."

Omar N. Bradley and Clay Blair, *A General's Life* (New York, 1983), 133, quoting Bradley.

Stephen E. Ambrose, *Eisenhower* Vol. I (New York, 1983), 418, quote.

Longmate, 22, booklet on "GI behavior" in England, by Eric Knight; 33, Eisenhower "out of a hole" belief of GIs.

Margaret Mead, "The Yanks in Britain", *Current Affairs*, 11 March 1944, No. 64, ABCA. Yanks "serious wooing."

Brian Dunning, BBC editor, article about Margaret Mead in WWII Britain, *The Plane Dealer*, (Cleveland, Ohio), 21 March 1992. Reported in *SHAEF Communique* #27, 15 December 1993, William C. Lahman, editor. (SHAEF Veterans Association, 2230 South Overlook Road, Cleveland Heights, OH 44106). Mead, in 1942, "was sent to England by the U.S. Committee for National Morale." Mead's third husband was an Englishman, Gregory Bateson.

Longmate, 33, quoting General Eisenhower; 261 "women scarce in western frontier."

Reynolds, 208, "GI Pro-Kit Cream."

Alma Lackey quote, ABC News *20/20*, "They were so polite."

Longmate, 285, "quadruplets."

Pamela Winfield, *Bye Bye Baby: The Story of the Children the GIs Left Behind* (London, 1992), 177-82, includes "useful addresses" for offspring looking for GI fathers through TRACE (Transatlantic Children's Enterprise), WAR BABES etc. National Personnel Records Center, St. Louis, MO., may release some ex-GI information to searchers.

Phillip McGuire, *Taps for a Jim Crow Army* (Santa Barbara, 1983), 250, President Truman "equality in Armed Services."

Letter to the author from Nancy Harrington quoting a friend's experience, "father hid GI's letters."

Marriage By The Numbers   **Pages 20-38**

U.S. Army Cir. 41, HQ ETOUSA, AG 291.1. August 1945, C. Long, personal papers to marry overseas, "will not bring discredit to the Military Service," "no PX." War bride documents, IWM, London.

Juliet Gardiner, *'Over Here': The GIs in Wartime Britain* (London 1992), 142, GI's three "wives."

British Dual Nationality (1 January 1949). British Consul, Washington, D.C., 22 July 1993, stated that, "A declaration made before a foreign official for the purpose of acquiring another nationality or for any other purpose did not affect the position in United Kingdom law."

Adjutant General Office, 26 May 1944, AG 291.1. Military Reference Branch, National Archives, Washington, D.C. Policy on wartime transportation to the U.S. for "the English" wife.

Vivien Harris, "Uncle Sam's Newest Daughters-in-Law", *Red Cross Courier*, May 1946, Vol. XXV, 18, GI has to "request transportation" for war bride; 18, "5,000 brides reached U.S.A. during the war."

Interview with Annie MacRae Stapp, 21 November 1985. Letter, 9 July 1992. *The Boston Daily Globe*, 2 August 1943, quote.

Churchill, *The Grand Alliance*, Vol. III, 680, training Royal Air Force (RAF) Cadets in the U.S.A.

Rupert Brooke, *The Soldier*, "that is for ever England."

Questionnaire, 21 February 1994, Gilbert Braithwaite.

Interview with Patricia Grimshaw Moran, 21 November 1985.

PART TWO   **1946: U.S. Army War Brides Operation**   **Pages 39-42**

Longmate, 326, "Invading armies" quote.

New York Times, 12 October 1945, 25, war brides "want ships."

War Brides and Their Shipment to the United States (U.S. Army War History, 1945-1946), Headquarters European Command: Office of the Chief Historian European Command. OCMH Manuscript 8-3. 1CA11, Military History, Washington, D.C., 15, war widows and others "ineligible" for U.S. transportation; 31, GIs "gripe" about Tidworth duty.

New York Times, 23 January 1946, 3, "bring back daddy"; 5 January 1946, 15, GI "priority" points for ships.

AGO 510, January 7, 1946. Military Reference Branch, National Archives, Washington, D.C., "son waiting at Le Havre."

U.S. Army Transportation Office, 14 Duke Street, London, W1. "Questionnaires." V. Long, March 1946, personal GI Bride travel instructions. War bride documents, IWM.

1946: The Brides Flotilla   Pages 43-44

Charlotte Johnson, "The Start of a New Day," *The Red Cross Courier*, Vol. XXV No. 9, March 1946, 5, lists the "nursery fleet" of ships. British "Utility clothing." Food and clothes were rationed in Britain until July 1954 when meat was "last product to be de-rationed," IWM. ETO Historical Division, USFET Transportation Division, Vol. XV, 30 April 1946, AG 332. "Since area activated, 36,908 applicants processed and shipped in 34 shipments through Tidworth." Colonel Thomas Houston headed the *War Bride Operation* at Tidworth, England. The first group arrived 22 January 1946. Supplies included 1,200 baby diapers and 200 cribs. Archives II, College Park, Maryland.

Good-bye, White Cliffs of Dover   Pages 45-49

U.S. Army, Circular 245 (11 August 1945), Travel Orders, Personal GI Bride papers, V. Long, February 1946, IWM.

New York Times, 28 January 1946, 22, "Waterloo Train Station"; 5 February 1946, l, "*Argentina* arrives in N.Y"; 10 February 1946, 16, "like attracted like."

ETO Historical Division, USFET Transportation Division Vol. XII, January 1946, AG 332. "Shipment of Brides," London Area Transportation Office, 48, "no war souvenirs or fire arms" allowed.

Ernest E. Salisbury, "The Immigration of G.I. Brides," *Monthly Review*, Department of Justice, (Immigration & Naturalization Service, INS) May 1946, 307, first-hand description of the "immigration process."

ETO Historical Div. USFET Transportation, Vol. X11, February 1946, AG 332. "First Bride Ship: *S.S.Argentina*", London Area Transportation Office, 49, "Greatest human interest story."

Hello, New World   Pages 50-53

"Falling for the Yanks," ABC News 20/20, "down the gangplank," V. Long. Video, MGH 3458, Film records, IWM.

New York Times, 5 February 1946, 1, new "colonists" arrive.

War Brides and Their Shipment, 54, "ships busy sailing from different ports"; Table III, 56, number of brides and backlog. See Appendix C.

New York Times, 6 June 1946, 23, Dr. Friedman, "scabies, lice."

Los Angeles Herald, 27 May 1946, ex-GI Robert Porter's complaint.

New York Times, 30 May 1946, 24, quotes U.S. Army Transportation Corps, "no outbreak of infection on ships from Southampton."

Elfrieda Shukert and Barbara Scibetta, *War Brides of WWII*, (Novato, CA. 1988), 120, "babies died, *Vance*, May voyage."

U. S. Army, *War Brides and Their Shipment to the United States*, 44-47, "the *Zebulon Vance* and *Santa Paula* Incidents." During the 7 May 1946 trip of the *Zebulon Vance* from Le Havre to New York, "three children died en route and four more perished following arrival, apparently by some kind of an epidemic." Dependents who had been exposed to infection in the *Santa Paula* incident were "isolated at the 15th Field Hospital", France, but "no developments were observed."

"Results of Policy Change Following Incidents." Copy in SGS file 333.5/1. Vol. III, "Investigations Misc." 12 May-21 August 1946, 19-20. Despite rumors that babies died at Tidworth, this official record does not record any such fatalities. On 8 June 1946 the War Department ordered that "greater care be taken in separating any dependent suffering from acute communicable diseases." They were not to embark "until their condition allowed them to travel." ALSO, the "load percentage of each vessel" was restricted to "25 per cent of children under six years of age."

Jenel Virden, *"Good-bye, Piccadilly": The American Immigrant Experience of British War Brides of World War II*. University of Washington, 1992, 195, "crates of oranges" quote.

Washington Times Herald, April 1946. The "Inquiring Fotographer" [sic] asked who made "better wives?"

Military Reference Branch, National Archives, Washington, D.C., 23 February 1946, AGO 291, "hi-jack our boys."

Salisbury, INS Monthly Review, May 1946, 308, brides "would make real contributions."

London Daily Express, 25 January 1946, 9, Mrs. Roosevelt gives London war brides "pointers."

New York Times, 10 February 1946, 16, "knew their husbands longer." Elizabeth Valentine reported from London.

Vivien Harris, *Red Cross Courier*, May 1946, "reasons for early divorces."

British government, Parliamentary question 10, "callous disregard" to war brides, and lack of child support, Major Bramall, 11 October 1946. Foreign Office, 371/51622, Public Records Office, Kew, England.

Paul B. Zucker, "War Brides Project Ends," *Red Cross Courier*, February 1949, 28, "Army pleased with war bride assistance."

J. Harrison Heckman, *Memoirs of a Victoria Country Lad* (New York, 1976), 206, "ARC service provided by New York City Chapter."

PART THREE   GI Brides Look Back   **Pages 59-86**

A Bride's Guide to the U.S.A. (London, c. 1945), 15-16, "glossary of English/American terms."

London Sunday Dispatch, 20 January 1946, "U.S. is not Utopia." A report from New York City sent by John Hall.

Transatlantic Brides and Parents Association (TBPA) is a national organization with branches and postal members across the United States and Canada. It was started in Britain after WWII by the parents of war brides in order to get "cheap" transatlantic charter flights. The appendage "A British Heritage Society" was later added to the name.

Interview with Margaret Willis Garman, 21 November 1985, Vienna Virginia.

Interview with Eunice Isaac Upchurch, 4 December 1985, Vienna, Virginia; letter, 27 March 1992.

Interview with Doris Norley Amsbaugh, 21 November 1985, Vienna, Virginia; letter, 12 August 1993.

Interview with Joan Atyeo Walker, 6 December 1985, Vienna, Virginia; letter, 7 September 1992.

World War II American Red Cross clubs in London were listed in the *American Red Cross Map of London,* n.d., as follows:

Servicemen. Columbia; Eagle; Hans Crescent; Interstate; Liberty; Milestone; Mostyn; Rainbow Corner; Vandyke; Victory; Washington.

Officers. Duchess; Jules; Princes Gardens; Reindeer.

Women. Charles Street Clubs--one for service women and one for officers.

Reynolds, *Rich Relations,* 190, "ARC employed 29,000 (half as volunteers)." 1943-1944 British Reverse Lend-Lease paid 16 million pounds sterling for buildings, facilities, etc.

American Red Cross Clubs, June 1945, "thank you" letter to British volunteers in London area.

Hans Crescent ARC Club, 1944, Vera Cracknell.

M. M. Chambers, *Youth Serving Organizations,* 1948, 142, background of WWII United Service Organizations and its six USO members.

Questionnaire and letter, 4 April 1993, from Eileen Wright Karten.

Divorce   **Pages 87-88**

Virden, *"Good-bye, Piccadilly",* 1992, 207, divorce problems. 219, "1,500 divorces occurred in the U.K. out of 52,000 wartime marriages."

Questionnaire and letter, 27 June 1988, Jean Holder Carter.

War Brides Across America   **Pages 89-110**

New York Times, 20 January 1946, "Topic of the Times" editorial.
Questionnaire and letter, 11 February 1992, Doreen Timmins Kriegler.
Correspondence with the author in response to request placed in
TBPA "Together Again" magazine, February 1993.
Ada Dimmock Donellan, 27 April 1993.
Dorothy Sephton Ferguson, 4 May 1993.
Eileen Fordham Racy, 6 April 1993.
Iris Barber Batten, 23 March 1993.
Nancy West Harrington, 23 April 1993.
Doris Dark Riley, 22 April 1993.

PART FOUR   Remembering Yesterday   **Pages 111-135**

Winston S. Churchill, *Memoirs of The Second World War* (Boston,
1959), 305. "Alone", May 1941.
Women in the Forces. An emergency Bill, 22 May 1941, gave the
British Government "practically unlimited power over the life, liberty
and property of all His Majesty's subjects in Great Britain."
Questionnaires sent by the author and received from the following:
Dorothy Peers Crocus, 1 April 1992.
Olive Howe Taylor, 24 August 1992.
Daphne Fensom Scott, 9 April 1993.
Audrey Firkin Stern, 12 November 1992.
June Marston Harris, 9 August 1993.
Elizabeth Spirit Quinn, 12 March 1992.
Annette Bridges Grawey, 5 April 1993.
Joyce Howlett Cubley, 5 November 1992.

World War II Grooms   **Pages 136-140**

War Grooms. "I was a Male War Bride," 1949. Howard Hanks
motion picture comedy. Re-released by Fox Video, 1994.
U.S. Department of Justice, Immigration and Naturalization Service.
INS 1950 typescript, Table 9A, total number of "husbands." ETO Record
Group 1309, Archives II, College Park, Maryland.
Questionnaire and letter, 1 February 1994, John Spencer.

War Brides to Canada   **Pages 141-148**

Joyce Hibbert, *The War Brides* (Toronto, 1978), 133. By 31 December 1946: 47,783 war brides had entered Canada. Of that number 44,886 were British brides.

Rebecca Priegert Coulter, "WWII War brides" *The Canadian Encyclopedia*, Second Edition, Vol. IV, (Alberta, Canada, 1988.) Canadian military policy regarding overseas marriages.

Questionnaire and letter, 9 June 1992, Mary Boyle Leon.

Questionnaire, 23 August 1992, Daphne Butcher Raven.

Congress Passes Bill to Admit Fiancées   **Pages 149-151**

June 29, 1946, Congress passed *Public Law 471*, allowing alien fiancées and fiancés to enter the United States.

New York Times, 6 May 1946, 18, "temporary visas" to foreign women engaged to GIs; 25 June 1946, "Fiancées Act."

Long, *World War II Pilgrim Brides from Britain*, 1989, 88-90, Joyce Curnow Hinze shared her story as a "fiancée."

PART FIVE   **Back To Blighty**   **Page 153-155**

Southampton Southern Evening Echo, 26 September 1986, 3, "first visit back" in 40 years.

New York Times, 29 September 1986, 1, Terry Trucco, reporter, "300 War Brides Go Home, to Tea and Tears"; Dame Vera Lynn photograph.

Dr. Jan Stovold, Imperial War Museum (IWM), *GI Bride Project*, 26-29 September 1986. Dr. Stovold and her associates interviewed Olive Cakebread Cherrington, Janet Westnutt Kovac, Eunice Isaac Upchurch, Vera Cracknell Long and many others attending the GI Brides Reunion in Southampton, England. All taped interviews are in the Department of Sound, IWM, Lambeth Road, London, England.

Peter and Keith Ashton. *Hampshire and the United States* (Southampton, 1986), 45. In 1945 a plaque was dedicated in Southampton: "World War II Headquarters, 14th Major Port of the U.S. Army". In addition to the nearly two million U.S. soldiers who passed through Southampton, 300,000 American tanks, trucks and other items of heavy equipment, 21,000 railway locomotives and ten million tons of cargo passed through the port.

Shakespeare, Sonnet 30, "remembrance of things past."

London Daily Mail, 27 September 1986, 5, war bride widow dies, "it was where she wanted to be."

Peter and Keith Ashton, 102. "The Bells of St. Mary's." The song dates from World War I and was written by Douglas Furber (lyricist) and an Australian, A. Emmett Adams, when they heard the bells sounding across the water of Southampton Docks. As the title song of a film by the same name it was a World War II hit for Bing Crosby.

"Falling for the Yanks", ABC News *20/20*. Video logged under MGH 3458, Department of Film, Imperial War Museum, London. Gwen and Audrey Bradley: two of three sisters who married Yanks. Alma Lackey: "extremely lonely." Olive Cakebread: four years in the Land Army.

"Exciting Encounter," *Together Again*, TBPA Magazine, Pat Morgan, editor, February 1987, 9, "Dame Vera Lynn" concert in Southampton.

World War II Veterans: 50 Years On   **Pages 161-163**

Pete Johnstone, *The Nation Gives Thanks: D-Day Landings 50th anniversary* (Portsmouth), 1994, 15, Eisenhower "let's go". 4 June 1994, Garden Party hosted by Malcolm Rifkin, Secretary of State for Defence, Southwick House, Hampshire, historic site of D-Day planning.

World War II men and women who served in SHAEF (Supreme Headquarters, Allied Expeditionary Forces) or ETOUSA (European Theater of Operations, U.S. Army Headquarters). June 1994, D-Day commemorations held on Allied invasion beaches:

GOLD   Western British beach
JUNO   Canadian beach
OMAHA Eastern U.S. beach
SWORD Eastern British beach
UTAH   Western U.S. beach

V-E Day commemorations, 8 May 1995. At Rheims Cathedral, British and American SHAEF veterans 50th anniversary memorial service. Premier of "The War in the West," a cantata by Carolyn Kizer, music by Owen Burdick.

Clipping from Elsie Schummer, "Mike at The Red School House in Rheims, France on V-E Day."

SHAEF War Brides   **Pages 164-170**

Questionnaire sent by the author and received from the following:
Elsie Cayless Schummer, 31 May 1992.
Alva Bromley Reeves, 27 February 1992. Stephen Decatur and William Lloyd Garrison, "my country" quotation.

Pages 171-189

William Allen Hearne, letter 17 March 1992, widower lovingly tells about his war bride, Kathleen Adkins Farrell Hearne.
Audrey Jiggins Peters, 26 February 1992.
Joan Moore Petersen, 1 March 1992.
Eveline Ruby Clark Roy, 20 June 1992.
SHAEF French Bride. Questionnaire and letter, 12 May 1995, Claire Laumonier Hill.

Cheerio!   **Pages 191-196**

Letter to the author, 9 January 1994, Hazel Raeburn Garrison. Rae, born in Plymouth, Devon, served in the ATS during WWII and married Cecil Garrison, U.S. Army. She wrote her "Ode" to the war brides, 30 July 1980.
Walter Prescott Webb, *The Great Frontier*. By the late 19th century, America's western frontier had "disappeared." Webb wrote about different kinds of American frontiers; "mighty ocean," the Atlantic.
Shukert and Scibetta, 58, Colonel Floyd Lyle, "Welcome" to America.
Frederick Marquis, Lord Woolton, 30 March 1946, aboard the *Queen Mary*. Advice to brides.
V. Long. Personal *Queen Mary* papers, "Lord Woolton" quote. War bride documents, IWM.
Tony Molloy, *Bushy Park At War, D-Day* (London, 1994), 19, "Wooton Pie," quotes *Readers Digest*, "Do you remember the Forties?" booklet.
Winston S. Churchill, *The Grand Alliance*, 14 June 1941, 688-89, "Action this Day," Prime Minister "to Lord Woolton."
Hilda Cracknell Prouse, personal papers from Charles Guy Fulke Greville, Earl of Warwick, 8 March 1944, "rabbits."
Reynolds, *Rich Relations*, 415, "happily?"
Lacey Baldwin Smith, *This Realm of England, 1399 to 1688* (Lexington, Massachusetts, 1983), 313, John Locke "inalienable rights."
Shukert and Scibetta, 4, Radcliffe College research papers.
"Daisy . . . all for the love of you!" written in 1892 by Harry Dacre. "Daisy Bell" was the inspiration for "A Bicycle Built for Two."

EPILOGUE   **A War Baby Remembers**   **Pages 197-199**

Letter to author, 19 January 1997, Christine Brooks Hopson.

BIBLIOGRAPHY

Ambrose, Stephen E. *Eisenhower: Soldier, General of the Army, President-Elect, 1890-1952,* Vol I. New York: Simon & Schuster, 1983.

American Red Cross. *The Red Cross Courier.* Washington, D.C.: Vol. XXV, May 1946.

Ashton, Peter and Keith. *Hampshire and the United States.* Southampton, England: Keywords Services, 1986.

Barbour, Philip L. *Pocahontas and Her World.* Boston: Houghton Mifflin Co., 1970

Bradley, Omar N and Blair, Clay. *A General's Life.* New York: Simon & Schuster, 1983.

A Bride's Guide to the U.S.A., British Good Housekeeping Magazine and the United States Office of War Information, c. 1945.

Brooks, Stephen. *Bomber: Strategic Air Power in Twentieth Century Conflict.* London: Imperial War Museum, 1983.

Burton, Elaine. *What of the Women: A Study of Women in Wartime.* London: Frederick Muller Ltd., 1941.

Chambers, M. M. *Youth-Serving Organizations.* Washington, D.C.: American Council on Education, 1948.

Churchill, Winston S. *Memoirs of The Second World War.* Boston: Houghton Mifflin Co., 1959.

_____. *The Second World War: Their Finest Hour,* Vol.II. New York: Viking Penguin Inc., 1985.

_____. *The Second World War: The Grand Alliance,* Vol.III. Boston: Houghton Mifflin Co., 1985.

Costello, John. *Virtue Under Fire.* Boston: Little, Brown & Co., 1985.

Coulter, Rebecca Priegert. "WWII War Brides." The Canadian Encyclopedia, Second Edition, Vol IV. Alberta: 1988.

Deighton, Len and Hastings, Max. *Battle of Britain.* London: Michael Joseph, 1990.

Dickens, Monica. *An Open Book.* New York: Mayflower Books, 1978.

Fitzgibbon, Theodora. *With Love: An Autobiography 1938-1946.* London, Centry Press, 1982.

Furer, Howard B., ed. *The British in America, 1578-1970: A Chronology and Fact Book.* Ethnic Chronology Series Number 7. Dobbs Ferry, N.Y: Oceana Publishers, 1972.

Gardiner, Juliet. *'Over Here': The GIs in Wartime Britain.* London: Collins & Brown Ltd., 1992.

Giles, Karen. *War Brides: An examination into the social impact of the Second World War emigration of the GI War Brides.* Thesis, Kingsthorpe, Northampton, England. 1992.

Hale, Edwin R. W. and John Frayn Turner. *The Yanks Are Coming.* New York: Hippocrene Books, Inc., 1983.

Heckman, J. Harrison. *Memoirs of a Victorian Country Lad.* New York: Stinehour Press, 1976.

Hibbert, Joyce. *The War Brides.* Toronto: New American Library of Canada Ltd., 1978.

Hough, Richard and Denis Richards. *The Battle of Britain: The Greatest Air Battle of World War II.* New York, London: W. W. Norton & Co., 1989.

Hutchings, David F. *RMS QUEEN MARY: 50 Years of Splendour.* Southampton: Kingfisher Productions, 1988.

Johnson, David. *V-1 V-2: Hitler's Vengeance on London.* New York: Stein & Day, 1982.

Johnston, Mary. *To Have and To Hold.* New York: Temp Books, 1970.

Johnstone, Pete. *The Nation Gives Thanks: D-Day Landings 50th Anniversary.* Great Britain: Graphic Studio, H.M.S. Dryad, 1994.

Kahn, David. *Seizing the Enigma: The Race to Break the German U-Boat Codes, 1939-1943.* Boston: Houghton Mifflin Co., 1991.

Kennett, Lee. *GI: The American Soldier in World War II,* New York: Warner Books Inc., 1987.

Lee, Helene R. *Bittersweet Decision.* Lockport, N.Y.: Roselee Publications, 1985.

Longmate, Norman. *The G.I.'s: The Americans in Britain 1942-1945.* New York: Charles Scribner's Sons, 1975.

Manchester, William. *The Glory and the Dream.* London: Michael Joseph Press, 1975.

McGuire, Phillip. *Taps for a Jim Crow Army: Letters from Black Soldiers in World War II.* Santa Barbara, CA.: ABC-Clio, Inc., 1983.

McTaggart, Lynne. *Kathleen Kennedy: Her Life and Times.* New York: Holt, Rinehart & Winston, 1983.

Mead, Margaret. *The American Troops and the British Community: An examination of the relationship between American troops and the British.* London: Hutcheson, 1944.

_____. "The Yanks in Britain", *Current Affairs,* 64, ABCA, 11 March 1944.

Miller, John C. *The First Frontier: Life in Colonial America.* New York: Dell Pub. Co., 1966; reprint ed., Lanham, MD.: University Press of America, Inc., 1986.

Molloy, Tony. *Bushy Park at War, D-Day.* London: The Royal Parks, 1994.

Morgan, Kay Summersby. *Past Forgetting: My Love Affair with Dwight D. Eisenhower.* New York: Simon & Schuster, 1975.

Morison, Samuel Eliot. *The Oxford History of the American People,* Vol. I. New York: Mentor, 1972.

O'Hara, Peggy. *From Romance to Reality.* Ontario, Canada: Highway Book Shop, 1983.

Parrish, Thomas. *The Ultra Americans: The U.S. Role in Breaking the Nazi Codes.* New York: Stein and Day, 1986.

Plumb, J. H., Youngs, Frederic A., Snyder, Henry L., Reitan, E. A., and Fahey, David M. *The English Heritage.* St. Louis: Forum Press, 1980.

Reynolds, David. *Rich Relations: The American Occupation of Britain, 1942-1945.* New York: Random House, 1995.

Salisbury, Ernest E. "The Immigration of GI Brides", *Monthly Review,* May 1946.

Shukert, Elfrieda Berthiaume and Barbara Smith Scibetta. *War Brides of World War II.* Novato, CA.: Presidio Press, 1988.

Smith, Bradley F. *The Ultra Magic Deals: And the Most Secret Special Relationship, 1940-1946.* Novato, CA.: Presidio Press, 1992.

Smith, Lacey B. *This Realm of England, 1399 to 1688.* Lexington: D. C. Heath Co., 1983.

Virden, Jenel. *"Good-bye, Piccadilly": The American Immigrant Experience of British War Brides of World War II.* Thesis, University of Washington, 1992.

_____ *Good-bye, Piccadilly: British War Brides in America.* Urbana and Chicago: University of Illinois Press, 1996.

War Brides and Their Shipment to the United States. 1945-1946 (Frankfurt, 1947). Office of the Chief Historian, Headquarters European Command, U.S. Army, "Occupation Forces in Europe" series, MHI Library, National Archives, Washington, D.C.

Webb, Walter Prescott. *The Great Frontier.* Austin: University of Texas, 1964.

Wharton, Margaret. *Marlborough Revisited and the War Remembered: A G.I. Bride Looks Back.* Gloucester: Alan Sutton, 1987.

_____. *Recollections of a GI War Bride: A Wiltshire Childhood.* London: Alan Sutton, 1984.

Wicks, Ben. *Promise You'll Take Care of My Daughter.* Toronto, Canada. Stoddard Publishing Co., Ltd. 1993.

Winfield, Pamela and Brenda Wilson Hasty. *Sentimental Journey.* London: Constable Press, 1984.

_____. *Bye Bye Baby: The Story of the Children the GIs Left Behind.* London: Bloomsbury Publishing Ltd., 1992.

INDEX